HOW WE UNDERSTAND THE WORLD
A Modern Education

ALAN MACFARLANE was born in Shillong, India, in 1941 and educated at the Dragon School, Sedbergh School, Oxford and London Universities. He is the author of over twenty published books, including *The Origins of English Individualism* (1978) and *Letters to Lily: On How the World Works* (2005). He has worked in England, Nepal, Japan and China as both an historian and anthropologist.

He was elected to the British Academy in 1986 and is now Emeritus Professor of Anthropology at the University of Cambridge and a Life Fellow of King's College, Cambridge.

A Modern Education
Advice for Ariston

ALAN MACFARLANE

2018

CAM RIVERS PUBLISHING

First published in Great Britain in 2018

5 Canterbury Close
Cambridge CB4 3QQ

www.cambridgerivers.com
press@cambridgerivers.com

Author: Alan Macfarlane
Series Editor: Zilan Wang
Editor: Sarah Harrison
Marketing Manager: James O'Sullivan
Typesetting and cover design: Jaimie Norman

The publication of this book has been supported by
the Kaifeng Foundation.

© Alan Macfarlane, 2018

The moral right of the author
has been asserted.

All rights reserved. Without limiting the rights under copyright reserved above, no part of this publication may be reproduced, stored or introduced into a retrieval system, or transmitted, in any form or by any means (electronic, mechanical, photocopying, recording or otherwise), without prior written permission of both the copyright owner and publisher of this book.

For Ariston Shum, with my love.
Alan Macfarlane, 2015

Contents

	PREFACE: Why I Am Writing to You	9
1	What is Western Modernity and How Did it Happen ?	14
	AN ENGLISH EDUCATION	27
2	Society and Power	29
3	Play and Performance	47
4	Head and Heart	63
5	Spirit and Character	78
	A WIDER WORLD: Consequences and Comparisons	97
6	Some Ways in Which Education Shaped the English World	98
7	English and Continental European Education	121
8	English and Chinese traditional Education	137
	CONCLUSION	150
9	Some Benefits and Costs of Modernity	151

PREFACE

Why I Am Writing to You

DEAR ARISTON,

You are still very little, but I have been asked by your father to explain something about the choices which lie ahead for you. He wrote to me in March 2015 as follows.

Dear Alan,
I have been spending much time in Oxford looking after Ariston, which I enjoy. Recently, I have been looking into a topic which I think may be of interest to you. I have always been fascinated with the modern history of China, so many ups and downs, twist-and-turns. So many possibilities of what could be.
    Specifically, I have the following questions:
1. 'Modernity' as a term is defined by the west. For most of the past 200 years, China has been trying to cope with that global trend. I would say we are still very much in that process. Many questions were raised in the mid 19th Century are still being asked today, and there have been no consensus.
    While being a leading civilization over the past thousand years, I wonder if there are features of our culture that prohibits us ever being able to integrate our society into modernity as it is defined today? If so, what are these?
2. China of today is of global relevance. If China is not going to integrate itself into modernity now, where is it going? How will its path pull the world off its trajectory? And what's the new trajectory likely to be?

3. Should we redefine modernity, given we live in a more multi-cultural and multi-religious world? Should we think of a new term? And what could that be, since so much is invested in the word?

To me these questions are fascinating. They raise the question of where China may be or should be going. As a result, where the world may be going.

I thought, given your background, you might be able to make some suggestions about part of the answer on these matters or point me in the right direction to find some answers.

Warm regards, Desmond

* * *

Dear Desmond,

Thank you for your questions. I am happy to try to give a brief and simple set of preliminary answers to them.

Thinking about how best to answer you simply, I thought that rather than repeating or summarizing what is already avail-able in five of my books (*The Origins of English Individualism, The Culture of Capitalism, The Riddle of the Modern World, The Making of the Modern World, The Invention of the Modern World*) I would try something different.

I have always been interested in how we change from being young children into adults. So I have started a project to show how this happened to me.

When I was about fifteen I decided to keep as much of the materials that related to my life — photographs, essays, letters, ephemera — as possible, as it might one day be interesting to look back over what had happened to me. I now have many hundreds of boxes of materials upon which I can base a detailed historical and anthropological account of how one English child was shaped into an adult. I am hoping to make all this available on the internet for future historians.

Here I will set my own experiences into a wider context by looking at how education, in the widest sense, teaches us how to be effective members of an adult world. Obviously my own experience is not typical or representative. Yet I believe that in essence it shows what happens to almost all British children, and is a continuation of a pattern that has lasted for hundreds of years.

What I shall describe is the process whereby I went from my early years in India, where I was born at the end of 1941, up to the end of my undergraduate course in history at Oxford University in June 1963.

The journey had six episodes. There were the six years, 1941-1947, during the Second World War and just after, spent in India with my parents. There were then seven years between 1948 and 1958 living in Dorset, in the south of England, mainly with my grandparents because my parents were in Assam working in the tea industry.

During this time I was sent off to a boarding 'preparatory' or Prep School. The school was called the Dragon School and located in north Oxford. There were a little over 400 boys and a few girls, aged between eight and thirteen. It was an unusually progressive and liberal school and many of the children were from academic families in Oxford and Cambridge. We lived for two thirds of the year in the school and I did not return to my home during the terms.

Towards the end of my time at the Dragon my family moved to northern England and so between 1955 and 1963 we lived in the middle of the English Lake District. It was a beautiful valley called Esthwaite Dale, where the poet William Wordsworth had lived. It was convenient for my next school, a 'public' (that is a boys-only, fee-paying, boarding) school, called Sedbergh in the Yorkshire moors. There I went in 1955 and stayed for almost five years until 1960.

This phase of my education, from infant to adult, ended with three years at Worcester College, Oxford, from late 1960 to the summer of 1963, studying history for a Bachelor's Degree.

An account of these stages, illustrated with several hundred photographs and scans of documents, is available separately as a companion volume called *Learning to be Modern*. There you will see in pictures this particular educational arch, from the last days of the British Empire through to the rise of the Beatles and Rolling Stones, looks like.

In this book I will give an overview of the ways in which British children are socialized, moving them from their family into wider society. The importance of the type of system I went through is underlined by the accident that the system was spread broadly by the British Empire (including to an early part of the Empire, North America) and is now being absorbed by many young people from China and elsewhere who are sent to British or American schools and universities.

The unusual nature of the system has been largely invisible to those who went through it, in other words the British. They took it for granted, just as I did for many years. Its peculiarity and essential features only come out when we look at British education in the mirror of other societies. So I have widened out the account at the end by looking at some of the reactions of people from Britain's nearest continental neighbours, the French. Moving out even further, I have included a comparison with a system which has some similarities, but also differences, the traditional Confucian educational system of China.

I end by returning to your question, Desmond. What is modernity and should China adopt it. I briefly look at some of the benefits of being 'modern' in the sense in which I define it, and also its costs. The decision of how much of our system you adopt is obviously up to you. But it may be helpful for you to have an analysis of what I think our system is and what it does. You are already starting along a certain path by beginning to educate Ariston in my old boyhood and university educational home, Oxford. This book will, I hope, help you and others who consider the British or American option to know what its main features are and the implications of selecting this path.

ONE

What Is Modernity and How Did It Happen?

PEOPLE SELDOM THINK much about the meaning of the word when they speak of the 'modern' (or 'modernity'). They often assume that it means 'recent,' a 'modern' house is one built in the last twenty years, 'modern' literature or history covers the recent past. So you could talk about 'modern' North Korea, contrasting it to 'pre-modern' France before the French Revolution. This is perfectly reasonable, but it is not the meaning I will be giving to the word.

Going a little deeper, people contrast a 'modern' nation like the United States or Germany with a 'pre-modern' country like Afghanistan or a number of nations in Africa. When questioned, what people usually mean here is a combination of characteristics. There are technological developments – the use of non-human power for industry, good communications technology, widespread use of cars. There are certain social characteristics – widespread education, relative equality of the sexes, an open system of social mobility. There is a particular type of political and legal system – power distributed fairly widely in some kind of 'democracy' and the 'rule of law.' The outcome of all this is that there is usually a certain degree of personal affluence and consumer choice.

This bundle of characteristics allows countries to be placed as 'more' or 'less' modern (or 'developed' in another terminology) and certain parts of a country more so than others (for example, Kathmandu is 'modern,' while much of Nepal is pre-modern).

This definition has its merits, even if some of the criteria clash and there are cases where a country is high on certain criteria – affluence and communications for example, and less so on others, women's rights or democracy. Where would Saudi Arabia be, for example, in terms of 'modernity'?

Yet when I use the term 'modern' in this book I am not using it in either of these senses, though there is some overlap with the second.

My understanding of modernity has gradually emerged in my thinking over the years, for it was never taught to me when I studied history or anthropology at university. It was only really when I travelled around the world and taught social anthropology for some years that I came to have an idea of another meaning.

There are four main human drives. One is towards material sufficiency, the production and consumption of goods, or what we would now call the economy. A second drive is towards power and domination, towards control of others through violence, physical and symbolic. This we call politics. The third is the area of the individual and society, social relations, kinship and reproduction. This is the social sphere. The final is the drive towards understanding and knowledge, belief and ethics. This is the realm of religion and ideology.

I learnt that in early societies, that is the ones which existed universally until about ten thousand years ago and which anthropologists term 'hunter gatherers' and 'tribal,' the basic characteristic was that these four aspects of human life were bundled together. There was no discrete sphere which we could label as 'Politics,' for power was a dimension of all relations and was largely based on family links. There was no area we could call 'Economics,' for exchange, labour and value, were all embedded within social relations and every transaction, gift or productive action also carried religious, social and political overtones.

Likewise one could not separate off 'Religion,' for all parts of life were simultaneously of ritual or symbolic importance, whether they were practical actions such as planting crops, or social relations such as parent-child ties.

Finally it was impossible to talk of 'Society,' that is personal relations and the nature of human groups without immediately bringing in power, belief and wealth, in other words politics, religion and economy.

I discovered that with the rise of civilizations around ten thousand years ago, a first separation occurred whereby, in the words of Karl Polanyi, the 'Economy' became what he called an 'instituted process,' a separable institution. You could analyse it as a discrete system, it was in Polanyi's term 'disembedded.'

At the same time, the development of writing allowed the emergence of instituted political systems – States – and instituted sets of beliefs with their attendant priests – Religion. Thus a first set of separations had occurred which made it possible for peasant, urban 'civilizations' to emerge, where individuals could start to act in ways which were explicitly religious, political and economic.

Yet this first major separation did not complete the division. While there were now 'The' Economy, Polity, Religion and Society, they tended to form into two pairs with strong overlapping interpenetration. In most civilizations until very recently, and in some world religions to this day (Catholicism, Islam, certain forms of Buddhism), Religion and Politics are not separated. In theory, a Catholic owes primary political allegiance to the Pope and a Muslim to Allah. Attempts to separate religion and politics, as in the American Constitution, India, Turkey and even France, have had mixed and partial success. Yet the struggle to enforce a separation goes on.

The second pair is Economy and Society. These also remained locked together in several ways in most parts of the world until recently. Until less than a hundred years ago, almost all economic production was organized on family lines. The farming household was the basic unit of production and consumption, with joint ownership and the oldest male as the director of operations. This was the situation in most of Europe, India, Africa, China and South America.

A related feature was that almost all occupations were determined by birth; the economy was based on social status. This was partly because in all these peasant societies in the Indo-European world there were four blood-based occupational groups – rulers-military-nobles, clerics-lawyers-literati, townsmen-traders-craftsmen, agricultural workers (peasants). Each was based on birth and blood and it was very difficult to move from one group to another, as, in the extreme form, the Indian caste system. The son of a noble would be a noble, the son of a peasant a peasant.

Max Weber frequently drew attention to the fact that the modern individualist and capitalist system, with rational law and participatory politics, could only emerge when people were 'set free' from their birth-given status positions within families. Only when they could control their own productive power, with full private property and individual rights against the wider group, could people be 'free' to transact in a market economy.

So as I examined the four major types of human society, I realized that 'modernity' was the stage when the first divisions of Politics/Religion, and Economy/Society were taken one step further, with four theoretically discrete spheres. This is what I mean by 'modernity,' the world of autonomous individuals who each, as individuals, embody and join together the four separate spheres, which otherwise are discrete. And possibly, as in the diagram below which summarizes the argument, we are now moving into another, post-modern, reality.

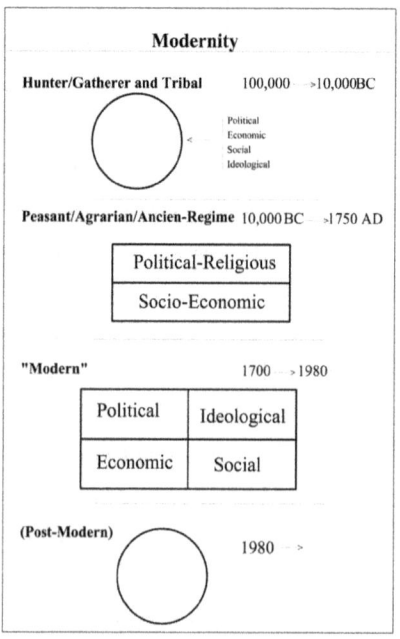

A MODERN EDUCATION

The lawyer and anthropologist Sir Henry Maine takes us to the heart of the question of modernity in his famous statement that 'The movement of the progressive societies is the movement from status to contract.' By 'status' he meant that relations are based on birth – mainly kinship. Whereas in modern societies birth does not determine everything, but 'freely' entered into 'contracts' through life is what determines our lives.

The first thing to say is that almost all known societies are based on status – birth. Modern Britain and America, the extreme examples, are highly exceptional. There was nothing inevitable about the process. Taking the basic feature, which is that in most societies your position through life is determined by your position in a kinship group, any anthropologist will tell you that almost everywhere a child never breaks away from the family. He or she remains a son or daughter, brother and sister. His or her life is determined in every dimension, from religion and politics to society and economics, by birth position and kinship relations.

What is extraordinary about modernity, and which allows the 'separation of spheres,' is that somehow the original kinship entity, the birth family, is in a sense destroyed. It is like splitting an atom and has the same huge effects of that intense moment of splitting of something which physicists had assumed was unsplittable, just as anthropologists might believe the family could not be split apart.

What has to happen is that the society and the family itself see it in their best interest that the individual is extracted from the bonds of kinship. At some point, perhaps gradually, perhaps dramatically, the individual is 'set free.' That is to say they have to enter into contractual relations even with their own family.

What has to happen is that the strongest of all relations, between a child and parent, has to be transformed from the assumed permanence and superiority-inferiority of the kind which is the keystone to Confucianism, Catholicism and almost all family systems, into one where the child becomes equal and separate from their parents, usually at an early age.

How can this possibly happen, since it seems to be against nature and against emotion, to be damaging to the parents who must effect it, and to the child who loses the warmth and protection of parents?

* * *

If this account has any value, it is because my own experience, while unique, is part of a much wider pattern. Although the content and methods of English education have changed hugely over the last thousand years, the deep structure or shape has remained largely unchanged. This shape has several features.

One is that children were sent away from their homes at an early age to be 'educated' or trained. It has always been felt that the best people to train the young are strangers, non-kin.

As far back as the records go, that is to Anglo-Saxon England about 1500 years ago, we find the custom that young people should sever their link with their parents and never return, except for holidays.

A classic account of this pattern is by the Venetian Ambassador Trevisano in 1497. He wrote that 'the want of affection in the English is strongly manifested towards their children; for after having kept them at home till they arrive at the age of seven or nine years at the utmost, they put them out, both males and females, to hard service in the houses of other people, binding them generally for another 7 to 9 years. And these are called apprentices...' He felt that if the parents had taken their children back when their apprenticeship was over 'they might, perhaps, be excused' but noted that 'they never return.' Instead, they have to make their own way in the world, 'assisted by their patrons, not by their fathers, they also open a house and strive diligently by this means to make some fortune by themselves.'[1]

What one was sent away to depends on the relative wealth and status of the family. The poor sent their children off to be servants in other people's houses and farms, where they would not learn a craft skill, but would relieve their birth family of the cost of upbringing. Servanthood is one of the great, unusual, and distinctive features of English society. It was widespread from the medieval period onwards and often involved very young people being sent off to distant homes. It is an institution which was not even found on the Continent, let alone in the peasant civilizations of Asia (with the exception of Japan). Many in the 'working class,' though this is an anachronistic term, that is perhaps the bottom third of the population, sent their children off as servants.

The young children would work as either household or farm servants and labourers and if they could save a little, might marry and then send off their children in turn. This phenomenon was transformed in the first half of the nineteenth century with industrialization and urbanization. The pattern remained in certain ways, that is the practice of sending poor children to work for others at eight or nine. Yet instead of becoming

---

1 *A Relation, or rather a true account of the Islands of England*, 1848, p. 24-6.

household or farm servants, they were sent to the mills and the mines.

At the next level up the social hierarchy, that is what one might call the lower and middle-middle classes, where the parents were a little independent and had some skills, there was a different pattern. These were the small producers, craftsmen, the smaller merchants and shopkeepers, the husbandmen and yeomen farmers. They had some capital and a business of some sort and they would send their children off to learn a trade or craft by being apprenticed to a skilled 'master.' Here the work for the master was meant to be combined with the transmission of the 'arts and mystery' of his profession. As with servants, this could apply to girls as well as boys, though I suspect that it was mainly for boys.

Thus, at the same age, that is between about six and ten, a child would go off to live with his or her master and learn a craft – shoe-making, blacksmithing, being a shopkeeper, working in some small enterprise. The child would work more or less for free (just getting accommodation, food, minimal clothing and perhaps a small gift of pocket money), but in return they had an expectation that at the end of contract – and this was indeed a formal contract, the young person would be qualified and could set themselves up in that trade, perhaps with some help from his master and parents. If the child went off, say, at eight, the apprenticeship might last for seven years or more.

Among the skills to be transmitted was some basic literacy and numeracy, partly taught in the household but also in elementary schools or in the evenings, which would be necessary for most small business and craft activities. Even a blacksmith had to keep accounts and write to people.

This widespread system of apprenticeship is again unusual and English. In most agrarian civilizations the child would stay in the home and learn their father's occupation by imitation and co-working. This I have seen with blacksmiths, tailors and farmers in Nepal and would have been the case for most of history in China, India and elsewhere.

The above was the pattern for the ninety or more percent of the population in England below the level of the professional upper middle classes, from the Anglo-Saxon period through to the industrial revolution. The pattern for the other ten or so percent was different.

The first prototypes of the English public schools emerged next to churches, Westminster was reputedly founded in 594 A.D. and Canterbury about ten years later. So it is clear that institutionally the boarding school is very old, some would argue the oldest continuous institution in English history. Many of the famous foundations date from the fifteenth century, and there was a burst of the founding of free grammar schools in the sixteenth, as with my boarding school Sedbergh. These were schools for the gentry, richer yeomanry and larger merchants. The Universities of Oxford and Cambridge, dating from the end of the twelfth century, were fed by such schools.

These schools and the old universities were set up to teach skills, useful for people who would later go into one of the non-manual professional groups – the church, law, education, civil service, upper ranks of the army and navy, upper levels of trade and commerce, the running of landed estates, and, from the eighteenth century, imperial administration.

The skills were partly social, the ability to speak and distinguish accents, cultural knowledge (including dead languages and authors), etiquette, taste and discrimination. Those who went through such education were separated from the less 'polished' mass of the population and the universities put a final burnish on them.

Yet there was also an intellectual component, a training of memory, logic, rhetoric, mathematics, linguistics, which could be useful as generic skills for any cultivated professional group. These schools were mainly for boys, but there were clearly numerous equivalents for girls from the eighteenth century.

These elite institutions, which had been as widespread in relation to the size of the population in the fifteenth century as they were in the eighteenth, grew again rapidly along with population and the increasing size of the upper middle class during the nineteenth century. In the middle of the century, the schools and universities were reformed and made into explicit machines to train those who would run the expanding British Empire.

At the top were the two old universities of Oxford and Cambridge, as well as the late medieval universities of Scotland. The less than ten per cent who had gone through the grammar school/ public school stream would now taper down to one or two percent attending university.

* * *

Such was the general shape of the English educational system in the long centuries from the Anglo-Saxon to the middle of the nineteenth century. Two or three outstanding and unusual features of this system are worth noting.

Perhaps the most important is the way in which by taking

education or training, or just growing up, out of the hands of the family, the world was changed. That all important separation between family and society, individual and society, society and economy, was built into the system.

This was the root of the autonomous and free individual, of the capitalist 'free' market, and of those deep separations of religion, politics, society and economy which constitutes modernity. This splitting of the atom of the family is painful and nearly impossible to achieve. It is an explosion or fission that has changed the world.

Secondly the fact that children learnt their culture from strangers meant that English schools, both in their formal structure and informal pressures, replaced the home as the locus of ethics and attitudes. Almost universally elsewhere, 'education' was to prepare the brain, or perhaps give some formal instruction in morals. But it was in the home that most of the moral and emotional education of children took place. In England, almost all 'education' took place after the age of eight in schools and amongst friends. Friends and teachers replaced the birth family. The education of body, mind, spirit and imagination was done outside the home. The home was for rest or 'holidays.'

By placing the education of all those above the level of wage labourers (servants) in the hands of formally and contractually appointed 'teachers,' whether the master in an apprenticeship,

or the master at school, or the Master of Arts at the University, it made it more likely that a more critical and objective teach-ing could take place.

The master of apprentices was skilled and had an incentive to improve his trade and be proud of his apprentices. The master at schools and university shared in the success of their pupils.

They were themselves trained a little in methods of education, literate, open to newer ideas which they could pass on. This contrasts with the strong tendency towards conservatism, the fear of the dangers of experimentation, and the mix of power, authority and discipline in home-based education.

Finally, a strong feature of the education at the top level of public, grammar and university education, was that it was generic. In a society where there were so many career ladders (army, navy, law, medicine, teaching, trade, manufacture, clergy, administration, running estates) children very often did not follow their parents' career schools and universities could not specialize.

An English Education

In order to give some depth and specific materials to this account, the next section of four chapters contains an anthropological synthesis of what I think happened to me in my education during the middle of the twentieth century. It is based particularly on my experience at the Dragon School, Oxford (1950-5), Sedbergh School, Yorkshire (1955-60) and Worcester College, Oxford (1960-3).

There are certain advantages and also dangers in using my own life and experience as a way of investigating English education. Among the advantages is that the experience is my own and deeply felt. Rather than having to rely on other studies, or other people's autobiographies, I can unite the different parts of a total experience that engraved itself on me and which I can examine from different angles. I can occasionally see the inner side of events and memories and piece together a continuous story over twenty-one years.

My experience was a typical example of a certain type of elite education of that period. Extreme in that I was educated in the top one or two percent of the British population at that time, the 1950s and early 1960s, who went for ten years to private boarding schools. These schools and universities were for this tiny minority, broadly representative. The Dragon School was more relaxed, innovative and liberal than many preparatory schools, but my public school (Sedbergh), was a slightly old-fashioned and remote boarding school for the period, so the two experiences balanced each other. The small Oxford college to which I went was also very much in the middle in terms of teaching and culture for the period.

It is important to realize that the patterns of teaching organization in elite schools were reflected in day schools too, particularly grammar schools, even though the experience was more intense in the boarding environment.

I was one of the last generation of an old pattern of being sent home from the Empire. Being a late case, the features were made more dramatically visible, a kind of caricature, partly by the dramatic changes which would alter much of the outward structure very shortly afterwards, partly because in trying to mould us into an effective elite – the rulers – the process was much exaggerated, explicit, more thorough, more organized than in the majority of schools. So it is more easily dissected – the skeleton is on the surface of the animal rather than buried within.

So I was neither typical nor representative. And this fact is emphasized by my own particular character and family background. Others would not necessarily have had such an intelligent and empathetic mother. Others were not identical to me in my character, a mixture of doggedness, self-confidence, anxiety, and a desire to hold onto my childhood certainties.

TWO

Society and Power

MY SEPARATION FROM my family became pronounced when I went off to my first proper primary school at the age of six and a quarter. There I found a world where my horizons were expanded in various ways and my self confidence was boosted. But the immediate effects on my relations with my mother are also visible. She wrote in a letter to my father:

> *Alan is still enjoying school, they play games and have break and then stories and some singing, I don't quite know where the actual teaching comes in ... He is a problem Alan, he is getting so difficult and rowdy and sticks out his tongue at me if I tell him anything. I sometimes feel I just can't control him. In fact I feel it several times a day! I know a good thrashing would do him good but can't bring myself to it, thou' he gets cuffed all day long. I suppose he's a normal small boy, and though I wouldn't have him otherwise I am too tired really to appreciate the fact.*

* * *

My mother's absence in India was a further distancing, so by the age of eight and three quarters when I went off to the Dragon School in 1950 I had already started to separate myself from my family. But now I was leaving home seriously, away for three months at a time and only returning home for rest in the 'holidays' for less than a third of the year.

I was sleeping, bathing, eating, playing and learning with strangers. I was subjected to communal boarding life with people I had never met and my parents or other family could not offer me any protection. It was the beginning of a process which would be repeated again five years later when I went to the north of England boarding public school of Sedbergh in 1955. And it would happen a third time when I went to Oxford University at the age of 18 as an undergraduate in 1960.

What happened to me in these thirteen years is a complex and lengthy story. The first thing to note is that while the events in the classroom and library, the training of my mind, was important, what was most important was what happened more generally through the whole boarding experience, an upper middle class variant of what happened when children of all classes were taken from their homes at a young age and turned from primarily being a member of a family to being first and foremost a member of 'society.'

As with all rites of passage, those going through it are best maintained in isolation, when the effect will be stronger. One central thing that stands out is that the boarding schools, and even Oxford, were during the term time semi-closed worlds. In many ways they fitted the description of what the anthropologist Erving Goffman calls 'asylums.' His work concentrates on prisons and hospitals, but much of it also applies to the institutions in which I was to spend three quarters of my life between the age of eight and twenty-one.

I found that in its central essence, that is as a multi level, stranded, and functional place where people ate, slept, worked and played in one place with the same set of people and where there was a good deal of control through various rules and some surveillance, so it was a kind of asylum.

Though the Dragon School with its large playing fields and river was very relaxed about our wandering about, the combination of our young age and being in the suburbs of a city meant that the boundaries had to be marked. We did not feel this as a constraint but just took it for granted – after all it was probably not very different from our home experience. Like well-trained dogs we would not wander off our small territory.

Yet the Dragon School had a number of boundary maintaining features which indicate its nature. Our letters home were sometimes monitored. We were not allowed to go out of school without special written permission, 'exeats,' and these were only given for short periods with parents or friends' parents. Parents were encouraged to take us to specified hotels. We tended to meet our parents outside the school gates. As far as I recall they seldom came into the school, except by accident as recounted in my mother's account. They did not routinely visit the dormitories, communal baths or classrooms.

Sedbergh was simultaneously more relaxed and stricter in its boundaries. We were now teenagers and hence less likely to get lost or molested, but also more likely to engage in more serious offences (in the eyes of the school) involving girls, drink, cigarettes or trespass.

In Sedbergh, however, the school had a perfect location since apart from the small town of Sedbergh and the village of Dent, the nearest towns were ten miles or more away. So we had a buffer zone round us and could expand in certain directions as we liked. Indeed we were encouraged to take off with our pack-lunches and to roam the countryside. So the school never felt closed or like an asylum. The open fells over which we roamed, the rivers where we swam and fished, all gave us a strong sense of openness and exploration.

Yet there were also very strict boundaries and it was at Sedbergh in particular that I learnt in detail about the way in which my life was to be filled with tiny, half-invisible, but terribly important lines which I could, or should not, cross.

There was a strict line between the school and the town. The main part of Sedbergh, though only a few yards away from my boarding house, was 'out of bounds' unless we had a particular reason for going up into town, such as buying school equipment. This was partly for our safety, the danger of the few cars and of being sucked into the whirlpool of drink, smoking, girls and other vices which might tempt us.

Within the house, space was carefully demarcated. A junior boy was not allowed to go into a study (except as a fag answering the call of the prefects) and a Junior Dayroom boy was not allowed into the Senior Dayroom. The half of the house lived in by the House Master, matron and servants was strictly out of bounds, as were other boys' dormitories. In the school itself there were form rooms one should or shouldn't enter, and playing fields for certain games. Entering another school house without permission was forbidden.

Moving up in the school led to a relaxation of some of the restrictions. Older boys could go into more junior parts of the house and would be more likely to get permission to roam further afield. Yet the intensity of the kind of asylum we lived in is shown by the strength of the symbolic boundaries.

The growing freedom we felt from the invisible asylum walls when we became school prefects in our last year was a preparation for the next phase of semi-bounded living at Oxford University.

At that time, in the early 1960's, there were still quite strict rules at Oxford. You could not be out of College at night after a certain time, roughly 10 o'clock. You could not go up to London for the night without permission. You were not allowed into ordinary pubs in the evening. You could not bring girls to your rooms after supper in the evening. You could not leave the University for more than a day or two without formal permission. You could not go into certain rooms or cross certain lawns. We were almost adults, on the verge of being released out into the world like long-term prisoners or monks, but still under the parental eye of the College and University until we finally 'went down.'

Alongside the rules about where we could go, our private space was bounded in other ways. At the schools, at first, we had almost no private space – from the start as boarders we lived communally and everyone could see the shivering, naked little boy in the bath, going to bed or in the changing rooms. I share the memory of Siegfried Sassoon who 'felt that the only life he could call his own was inside his play-box along with his tin of mixed biscuits.'[1] We were living a life almost completely in public in a very crowded space inhabited by strangers.

It was difficult to conceal anything. We did creep off to smoke, or eat illicit foods, in tree huts in summer. Yet there were conventions amongst the boys themselves which allowed them a tiny

---

1 Vyvyen Brendon, *Prep School Children*, 2009, p. 208.

bit of personal space. For the most part it had something of the feeling of like the famous description by Jeremy Bentham of a model prison based on a 'Panopticon,' where the warders were (in theory) watching one all the time. Yet though I remember the shock of the lack of privacy and loss of personal control over space, time and my body, I don't on the whole remember a sense of being watched all the time.

* * *

Many of the rules seem very petty and small, and the punishments, for example for being late into bed or running down the corridors or leaving one's clothes untidy, seem out of proportion to the gravity of the offence. Yet the proliferation of rules and the severity of punishment for their infringement, as in other asylums, reflect a perhaps accurate knowledge on the part of the authorities that they were sitting on a volcano. So all our lives were tightly disciplined and rule bound. And the rules were not only set by the school authorities, but the boys devised many others in order to control each other. It was an orderly anarchy, as described by many anthropologists. The written rules were few, yet the informal rules were many. The title of Foucault's book, *Discipline and Punish*, could well represent one side of boarding school life.

On the other hand the system also had a strong element of flexibility. Rules were for a purpose and if the purpose was better served by breaking or bending a rule, the ends could justify the means. Thus, much of the skill which led to success at school was the art of understanding the rules, and then bending and adapting them to one's own use. This was taught to us in all the formal games we played, but we also learnt it in relation to all the rules of life. For example, if one had an immense amount of work to do and felt exhausted, it might be legitimate to claim that one was sick and get a few days rest in the sickroom. Or if one was trying to write, as I did towards the end of my time at Sedbergh, one could ransack other writers for models, which were not always acknowledged.

So we learnt to internalize and respect rules, but also to question some of them, manipulate them, even break them. We learnt to realize how much of our life is constructed artificially and can be changed by an effort of will and ingenuity. We learnt to live in a world where there was constant evolutionary change going on. New things and ways had to be absorbed. The external world, particularly in the period of very rapid technological and social change between 1948 and 1966 when I was being educated, was changing rapidly and we had to absorb all this, along with a changing culture. In the midst of this we ourselves were changing, our bodies going through strange alterations, our emotions volatile and unpredictable, our minds suddenly interested in new thoughts and with new powers.

So we learnt the art of continuity with change, resisting unnecessary change in the conservative way that has often been noticed of schoolboys, dons and other members of semi-closed societies. We tried to keep things as simple as possible, but when a change made good sense then we incorporated it, often with the pretence that we were just re-inventing an older tradition. We came to learn through participation that there are complex webs of customs and rules which, we began to understand, have been devised for a purpose. We learnt that getting rid of an apparent anomaly may, in fact, reveal that it had a purpose and bring unpleasant unintended consequences. It is safer to leave things largely alone.

* * *

One of the techniques used at the Dragon, Sedbergh and even Oxford, to train us for our future lives was to arrange life in a series of parallel ladders up which we were encouraged to climb. There were intellectual ladders. The school forms were arranged in a long ladder with several dozen levels from Lower Five in the Dragon into which I first slipped, to Upper Sixth History (Clio) Sedbergh from which I graduated ten years later. The movement upwards was a long march. Twice a year or so there were exams and we were gradually toiling upwards towards a possible distinction of some kind.

Certainly as significant in terms of status were the games teams, from the fifth game or even lower, up to the First XV or First XI, depending on the sport. From the first, the masters were on the lookout for talent and we were spurred on to try to climb the ladder to win the respect of our peers – and, in my case, my sports-loving father. As well as the formal team sports – rugger, football, hockey and cricket – there were others, tennis, swimming, athletics among them, where we gradually moved upwards through teams and sets.

These shaded into more informal hierarchies in many of the playground games and hobbies, boys being ranked in marbles, conkers, five-stones and other annual crazes, as well as strength in fighting or facing pain. At Sedbergh the activities were different, running became paramount and the hobbies changed to fishing and walking amongst others. But there were still ladders.

Then there were hierarchies in drama, music, art and other activities such as chess. Those who played major roles in the annual Shakespeare or Gilbert and Sullivan events were given considerable status at the Dragon and those who excelled in public speaking and debating, or had a particular skill, for instance in archaeology or ornithology or mountaineering, were given extra status at Sedbergh or Oxford.

Another ladder and place where were disciplined was in relation to army training. There was none of this either at the Dragon or Oxford, but in the Sedbergh years the activities associated with the 'Corps' as it was called, or the C.C.F. (Combined Cadet Force) was quite dominant. And such preparation was to be encouraged because the regimentation, loyalty, unquestioning obeying of orders, the learning to give orders and to lead, all these were qualities which would be useful in many fields outside the army. Some would go on to be famous soldiers, but in 'civvy street,' someone who could lead a 'squad,' whether of young lawyers or young Ph.D. students was an asset.

I learnt from all this that life, as both my preparatory school motto, *arduus ad solem* (by striving, to the sun) and Sedbergh motto *dura virum nutrix* (a hard nurse of men) reminded us, was a constant struggle. One might be doing well on one ladder, but slipping on another. Nothing was assured or guaranteed. One might have rich parents, or a big strong body, or a good brain, but that was not enough. Only skill, concentration, commitment and effort would move one upwards and gain the esteem of teachers, other boys, one's parents and above all oneself. We were continually being watched, judged, examined, both by our teachers and our fellow students – formally and informally – and trying to prove ourselves.

There must certainly have been those who felt inadequate and unable to achieve much. Yet at both the Dragon and Sedbergh things were arranged so that even the academically middling, like myself, felt a certain degree of hope, and as we went through the school and automatically moved up in various ways, our self-confidence was boosted. Analysis of my school reports shows that my teachers were constantly writing that I was capable of good things, and often congratulated me on doing well. I was supported and pushed on by what now seems a genuine concern that I succeed as far as my abilities would take me, even if, as now seems evident, I was quite clearly classified in formal education by my teachers at the Dragon at least as middling.

* * *

Alongside this there was the equally important placing in hierarchies which were more structured in the sense that they did not depend on personal effort or ability, but placed people in sub-groups arranged in opposition to each other, or on a ladder. These structures included school houses, dormitories, 'suppers' and 'tables' (what time and with whom one ate). Special targets were being the captain of a team or, a minor target, a school prefect, but we all moved up these structured steps with age.

One strong feature of both the Dragon and Sedbergh, continued into Oxbridge, is the way in which our world was organised on age principles. All of these 'total' institutions were dealing with children and young adults who were changing very rapidly in a short period of time. My letters and other papers show the continuity of my character, but also the large gap between say a nine year old and a twelve year old, let alone a fourteen or sixteen year old. Our bodies, minds and emotions changed very rapidly and the schools had to make their teaching and their structures work for people going through these great transformations. So we were treated differently on the basis of our age.

We were also largely ruled through the mechanism of age. Many tribal societies, divide people into age sets who go through their lives with the same people and at different stages in life play, train, marry, have families, retire and die, often roughly in line with the famous seven ages of man or woman.

In the intense atmosphere of a closed boarding school a good way to keep control and enhance integration was by emphasizing age boundaries. This was done in many ways; the tables at which we sat for meals, where our classroom was, the house or dormitories one was in, a subtle expansion of privilege.

While age-grading was powerful at the Dragon, it seems to have been even more pronounced at Sedbergh. There was once again that sense of movement – starting with hardly any space, status or power as 'new boy,' then gradually growing stronger in every way until at the later age you were at the top.

Since not every one could be good at games or at work, the automatic elevation by way of the process of ageing was a compensation. Even a not very bright or sporty seventeen year old had a respect and status well above a brilliant and sporty fifteen year old. And any cheek from a much younger boy would quickly be punished.

The ancient art of divide and rule seeped into all aspects of our lives. The constant jockeying and confrontations between houses, sets, forms, dorms, age groups, kept the boys in a constant state of mild mutual antagonism and with separate interests. The lack of class consciousness and unity, of a consolidated 'we the pupils' against 'you the authorities' was a feature of school. We were unlikely to rebel, for each of the subsets of the school had different goals and different stakes in the status quo.

In many societies there is a heavy marking of the move from one age grade to another – at puberty, at first success as a warrior, at marriage, at childbirth. What is surprising in the English case is that is so little marked. Where was the puberty ritual at Sedbergh? In one way the whole five years was similar to the seclusion and indoctrination – often through suffering – of classic puberty rituals. Yet it was done over a long period, with subtle and gradual shifts continuous happening, and no single dramatic ritual marked the transition.

The big cross-country races, the special military parades and field days, the 'O' levels around the age of fifteen, the religious Confirmation Service about the same time, the moving from trebles to basses in singing, the being a head of a dayroom, the move from the under sixteen 'Colts' to upper sports teams, becoming a prefect, all were steps along the path from childhood to adulthood. And at home there were others – above all my purchase of my first motorbike at the age of seventeen.

But they were not all bundled together into one key turning point. And the sexual side, which is so marked in many societies, was hardly referred to at all. It was noted that we lost our treble voices, that our bodies expanded. Yet there was little discussion or obvious interest by the wider society as represented by the school in our development into sexual maturity. Indeed we were almost artificially kept away from all this. Being a single-sex school formally obliterated women from our consciousness. We were almost temporary eunuchs – muscular, mature, yet without sex. This was one of the many paradoxes and contradictions of this strange world of growing lads, who remained 'lads' until they went off to Oxbridge and suddenly became 'young gentlemen.'

* * *

While the Dragon was mainly about teaching us to live in a community away from home, the rules of communal living, the making of friends, how to co-operate and if necessary coalesce, Sedbergh began to teach us different skills, in particular how to accept and then assume authority, how to be ruled and how to rule.

In many ways the organization of the British public school and the British Empire were analogous. Both were attempted solutions to the problem of ruling indirectly, systems of the delegation of power so that people learnt to rule themselves.

A public school housemaster faced with fifty boys aged thirteen to eighteen, living an intense 'asylum' life had very few sanctions or ways of controlling the boys directly. He would find it best to appoint five or so trustworthy ('trusties') prefects who were given considerable, sub-delegated, powers, as in the feudal system upon which this was modelled. These prefectswould, in effect, have servants – fags – to relieve them of some of the humdrum duties such as cleaning shoes or cleaning their studies. Likewise, later in life, we might come to have 'servants', whether the numerous ones in the overseas Empire, or the secretaries, personal assistants, porters or gardeners of an Oxbridge College.

The prefects could punish with lighter punishments (drawing 'maps,' or detentions), and were even allowed, with permission, to beat younger boys. They were poised half-way between the master and the boys – boys themselves, they were able to represent their juniors, yet they could also represent the power of the masters to the boys. So they were like the native princes in India, or chiefs in Africa. They kept an eye out, administered local justice, and did much of the practical and day-to-day work of administration.

In the case of the school, this was perceived to have two advantages. For the housemaster it made the running of a house far easier. The house largely ran itself and the master's power was almost invisible in the true tradition of imperial power. The 'natives' appeared to be ruled effortlessly. There was no basic antagonism of the natives against the ruler, as in so many empires, since the natives were partially co-opted into the role of ruling themselves and each other, as often happens in prisons, hospitals or other institutions.

The second advantage was that the schools felt (justifiably) that they were teaching not only academic subjects but also an ability to lead and rule responsibly. A prefect had to have authority as well as power in order to be effective. He should be trusted, liked, respected, not an arbitrary, selfish or cruel despot. So as I grew through the system in Sedbergh I was learning how to become a ruler of my juniors.

The art of ruling people through authority rather than naked power has to be learnt. Yet I found it not too difficult to move from being a servant and powerless, to being a ruler of servants and, within limits, having some power over others. It seemed a natural progress. I found the gradual awarding of small signs of privilege, the unbuttoned jacket of a house prefect, the umbrella of the School Prefect, the increasing private space and personal initiative in work, were all a great pleasure.

So we learnt deference to authority and how to exercise power without revealing the iron hand behind the glove. We had learnt the customary norms and values of our culture, when hitting was allowed, when a white lie was permissible, how humour could deflect tension, how to make two people feel they had received justice and no one's pride had been hurt, how to end feuds, how to encourage people to do their best by leadership and enthusiasm. In other words we had learnt all the arts of rhetoric and dispute settlement which a good African chief or elder needs in his tribal society. These are the arts of face-to-face leadership which public schools were meant to teach.

These are nowadays somewhat derided skills. Yet they came in useful later. For example, being Head of a Department or Chairman of a Faculty in Cambridge, when everyone was more or less equal and some much older and more experienced than myself, and where I had no sanctions, tested what I had learnt. Without my early Sedbergh training I am not sure I would have managed as easily. The fact that the British Empire, and now the British Government, tends to be run by old public school boys (and occasionally girls) is perhaps not so surprising.

* * *

The way in which most societies are organized is based on what anthropologists call a segmentary lineage model. That is to say, there are levels of splitting where units on the same level are the enemies, but may also be united at a higher level. To take the case of a boy such as myself in my third year at Sedbergh. I was opposed to the three other boys in my study – for instance we might quarrel mildly about the pin-ups or the music we wanted to play. But if my study and its honour were impugned, I stood with the others against other studies. These studies were in competition with each other, but if the prefect above or dayroom boys below attacked a particular study, we would unite. Then, while opposed to other parts of Lupton House, if the house was in its many competitions with other houses, we would join as Luptonians. But if town boys or some outside force attacked Evans House, then we would be united as Sedberghians. And as Sedberghians we contested with Rossall or Uppingham, but in the holidays I united with my public school friends against non-public schoolboys. But in the trenches or supporting the English football team (though I tended to support Scotland where I could), we were English or British versus the rest.

So our identities and loyalties were multi-level in the same way as they were to be at Oxford or later in my life at Cambridge. Because of the house, Sedbergh segmentary structure was stronger than at the Dragon. Sets and classes at the Dragon, as at Sedbergh, were never more than functional groupings, with little sense of loyalty or identity. You fight with the people you eat, play, and share sleeping space with, not with the people you just study with. The house spirit was an effective way of binding us into wider loyalties and creating an artificial identity of a kind which was neither ethnic nor national, but based on temporary affiliations.

A MODERN EDUCATION

* * *

It is obvious that any institution such as a boarding school will manufacture a number of symbols both to instil identity, to create differences from others, and to show differential status. One powerful source of identity and expression of the ideals of Sedbergh school, as at the Dragon, was the set of school songs. The founding myths and history were encapsulated in 'Floruit Sedberghia,' which we had to learn by heart and sing on major occasions.

One verse and refrain from the Dragon School Verse:

> Let us always keep heart in the strife
> While our wickets or goals are defended,
> For there always is hope while there's life,
> And the match isn't lost till its ended!
> But whether we win or we lose,
> If we fight to the very last minute,
> The intent of the game is always the same –
> To strive that the Dragon may win it!

At Sedbergh, the refrain to the song which we sung every year to celebrate the ten mile cross country run which all boys should, at some time, run was:

> Strain and struggle, might and main,
> Scorn defeat and laugh at pain;
> Never shall you strive in vain
> In the long run!

Then there were flags and crests. The school had a flagpole where the school flag fluttered, showing the heraldic devices adopted by the school (though not formally and officially granted until the 1980s). It had the supposed coat of arms of the founder Roger Lupton – including the ferocious wolf's head with a symbolic link to the founding of Rome and the 'hard nurse of men,' i.e. being suckled by wolves. The school flag was brought into the Remembrance Day celebrations and the school crest was something a School Prefect could wear on his jacket as a badge of honour.

Then each house had a special colour – Lupton was austere, black and white, while Sedbergh with its muddy brown was puritan and Spartan. And each house had a flag and a crest. Lupton could proudly fly the wolf's head (occasionally replaced by pyjamas at the end of term). So each house had a kind of totem, and this set up the system of totemic oppositions.

Then there was other clothing – the games uniform of brown and blue, the kilts which many of us wore (including myself), as a symbol of our Scottishness, the ties and caps, the rolled umbrellas, the doing up of buttons, army uniform, the wearing of shorts until the 1970s.

THREE

Play and Performance

GIVEN THE HUGE emphasis on the physical disciplining of children, the games, sports, toughening up and occasional physical punishment, it is clear that much of my school life was to do with toughening the body. This made sense in a world of pre-modern medicine, inadequate heating (or cooling), and limited food in many remote parts of the globe. This meant that the body had to be really tough and inured to pain to survive.

We should strive hard to be good at games, and respect those who were. But again we should keep this in moderation. Modesty in our achievements, putting more emphasis on commitment and effort rather than attainment, was encouraged. Sport and games were a necessary part of growth, but they could be over emphasized.

I should learn a certain style of deportment. Of course, almost all children were taught these things at home or at school, but we were being groomed for an elite bodily discipline. Thus there was sometimes overt but often indirect instruction on how to swim, how to run and jump, how to walk, how to sit, how to sleep, how to go to the toilet, how to wash and keep yourself clean.

I should learn to be nimble and balanced, poised and resilient.

I should learn how to eat properly and to speak properly – that is, speak appropriately for my social background. But equally I should not scorn those who did these things differently.

I should learn how to shoot, how to boat, how to ride a bike and many other practical applications of bodily skills. I was to learn how to face pain and sickness without flinching, how to accept nakedness and being with others when I was naked, or to dress myself up and play a part when needed.

The most important can roughly be termed 'play,' serious play as well as frivolous. That is the art of inter-acting with other boys to learn associational skills and how to face life through simulated battles, contests of mind and body. Here again we can divide the subject into two: formal, organized, school sponsored games on dedicated play areas, team games like football and confrontational games like tennis. And the other kind, more informal play amongst ourselves, on the playground and in our boarding houses.

* * *

At the Dragon there were two autumn games which were special and deserve separate treatment, conkers and marbles. Marbles was the more interesting and obsessive. The main action took place along the fence where up to fifty little boys would have their 'stalls,' setting up little pyramids, or a line of spaced marbles.

The 'pricing,' ie. setting of the intersection between risk/reward was done by working out how far the person had to throw from. The distance varied from a few feet, if one had just put one or two common marbles to up to 50 yards if the target was a huge spiral of the best kind. Only a brilliant shot could get these – someone armed with a large bag of marbles. In pursuit of one of these whole fortunes could be gambled and won or lost.

Playing marbles required a combination of physical dexterity and skill, temperamental control and perseverance, self-confidence and self-belief. The whole process combined several human desires. Aesthetic appreciation – the miraculous colours and shapes. Greed and avarice. The pleasure of making collections. The honing of skills. The excitement of the hunt. The pleasure of taking risks and succeeding. Concentration and skill.

Playing marbles taught me the assessment of risk, the quantification of chance and probabilities, scales of comparison between valuables, the function of bargaining and exchange, the social bonds created through competition, the delights of acquisition, sharing and abandoning valuable objects, competition for status in a hierarchy, the laws of supply and demand (sometimes a boy would flood the market and a certain kind of marble would rapidly drop in value). I also learnt when to hoard and when to distribute, conspicuous consumption and value given through giving things away.

Ultimately it taught me how to lose without losing myself, how to distance myself from objects, how to come to terms with winning and losing and, most importantly, the transience of worldly goods and their ultimate worthlessness.

All this was a child's world – and largely limited to school. The rules were worked, out by the boys, and their observance was in our hands. This was one of its most important features – marbles constituted an 'informal' economy and politics, which beside the formal one of the school. Playing it taught self-reliance, self-organization, the ability to police and adjudicate without the use of formal sanctions. It taught trust and the value of contracts. All these were very useful skills for supposed future rulers of an extended Empire with a minimal enforcement capacity, or life in the city or any professional occupation.

* * *

Playing games used to be strongly encouraged in most schools. This is partly to strengthen the muscles and to use up surplus physical energy. Team games are also believed to improve social skills. The essence of a team game is to balance selfishness, the desire to shine and triumph, with sociality, the desire to make one's team win. This balance is also one of the most difficult things to achieve in much of social life. When to keep the ball and when to pass it to another is an art which stretches out into many of our activities. The balance between co-operation and self-assertiveness is well taught within the structured environment of the rules of a game.

It is also believed that games enable people to learn how to demarcate their lives. While the game is on we abide by certain rules. Then the whistle blows and we move immediately back into another reality outside the temporary suspension of the rules of normal life. Learning how to handle defeat (it took me some years not to weep bitterly after losing a game), and feel relaxed with someone who has outwitted or outplayed you, is an important art.

Likewise the subtle art of playing within the rules, but using as much leeway ('sailing close to the wind') and skill as possible, is one which is handy in almost every branch of later life. You have to learn the rules of your trade or occupation, but if you just stick to these without creative thought then you will end up as mediocre. If you break the rules and are caught the result is even worse. How can you keep to the rules yet excel? Skill, personal tricks, long training and perceptive observation of others are required. The concept of 'spin,' which makes the ball behave in odd ways in cricket, and disguises the real motives of politicians when they deal with the public, is one example of this.

People enjoy playing games because they like to compete and dominate; to play, strive, outwit, win, are all important survival tools. But there is more to games than this, particularly team games. Members of a cricket, football or bowls team play together, often socialize together and either create or express their friendship in this way. Friendly rivalry in the squash court may also cement friendship. Matching minds and bodies, or depending and sharing with other members of the team, both give great satisfaction. Friends play together and the stress on learning games at school is also meant to be a lesson in friendship. Like friendship, play is not directed to a practical goal. 'It is just a game,' but to refuse to play is a rejection.

Games shaped the person I am and much of my adult life, both in work and leisure, has been an application of what I learnt in those early hobbies and games. They have clearly been one of the single greatest influences on my personality. So I ran and jumped and kicked and batted and threw vigorously for ten years. Fortunately some natural ability plus the early training from an uncle, combined with determination, meant that I was reasonably successful, though not outstanding.

And of course, as well as the most important games, team

games, there were also many oppositional games, tennis, fives, for some golf etc., which taught other skills.

* * *

Formal public performance was encouraged in order to second main area was encouraged in order to stimulate creativity, ingenuity and self-expression, to teach self-confidence and the ability to lead others. This encompasses a large emphasis on art, music, drama, dancing, debating and oratory. All these were given a high emphasis during our schooling. For those who excelled in any of them they could lead to a career in politics, drama or the media.

There was a high emphasis on oratorical skills at both my boarding schools; rhetorical skills, debating skills, and generally encouraging public performance in public spaces. One day one might head a company, be a barrister, be a cabinet minister, command a ship or regiment. All these required not only self-confidence and leadership skills, but often the ability to persuade others through speech. And humour, particularly irony and satire and buffoonery were all very important tools. A lot of the skills were teaching us how to negotiate with others and to face the world.

A brief illustration can briefly from my first encounter with this important art, a tradition which continued at Sedbergh and Oxford. There was a formal debating prize at the Dragon, called the Fitch Prize. I never contended for this but went to some of the debates. Here I shall give the topics chosen for my first three years, taken from the reports each term which give the names of the boys, their subjects and a report on parts of their speech and how they were classed. A prize could be won in each term, but no one could win more than one prize in a year.

The topics in my first year were: Prep., Korea, Christmas Presents, Holidays, Swimming, Liberal Party, Anti-nationalization of Sugar, Classics to be optional, What School Subjects should be taught. In my second year: The advantages of phonetic spelling, Christmas Presents, Camping Holidays, Trying to be helpful, Shakespeare, Cats, Punctuality, Holidays, Bad habits of the Staff.

In my third year (the first term missing – only two competitors), Fox-hunting, Learning foreign languages at school, The British workman, The ideal Schoolmaster, School rules and Punishments, Relatives, India, Was the Coronation in London worth it? Space Travel Possibilities, Mucking about.

In my fourth year the topics were: The pleasures of camping, the attractions of farming, (second term, Easter 1954, report missing), History is bunk, Railways, The History of Flying. In my last year the topics were: The folly of trying to reach the moon (the only competitor in the first term because of flu), The value of international sport, Myxamatosis, Birds, The H Bomb, The Colour Bar.

Two themes seem worth noting. One is that the occasion could be used to make amusing criticisms or suggestions about the school – as in 'The Ideal Schoolmaster' and 'School rules and Punishments' and 'Bad Habits of the Staff.' There was also also quite a serious interest in politics and world events – the nationalization of sugar, Korea, the Colour Bar, the H bomb and other topics.

* * *

As we were being trained to be members of society more generally, one of the central skills we had to learn was to join with others in associations, clubs and small societies. So from the start of my schooling, and very fully from my preparatory school, we were encouraged to form many kinds of association or club, some sponsored by the school, others we set up ourselves. This would foreshadow, after being encouraged even more at public school and becoming one of the most important parts of our university education, a world where as professionals we would find much of our pleasure, and perhaps our useful contacts, through clubs and associations. These clubs taught us organizational ability, responsibility and leadership, learning to trust others and work and play together in a non-family environment.

As they are so important, I shall briefly illustrate them from the two ends of the education, the preparatory school and University. One of the Dragon clubs was gardening. The Dragon had allowed the boys to dig up part of a bank near the road opposite to School House and above the sports sandpit. Here we were encouraged to do a little gardening, planting both flowers and vegetables. I remember that I was quite keen and had a small patch with carrots, the great standby, and perhaps some mustard and cress. I don't remember ever winning any prizes.

Another club was for chess. Chess was considered very important at the Dragon from the founding of the school. Both the founder and his son had played chess for the county and it was widely recognized that it was extremely good for the brain.

In the Term Notes for Christmas 1952 it is mentioned that the first ever award of ties (special prizes) for chess was made, putting it on a level with other serious sports and games. The chess team regularly appeared in photographs in the school magazine, *The Draconian*.

There were many lively clubs at Sedbergh, several to encourage us to enjoy the magnificent local scenery, but the importance of clubs reached its peak at university. University is where many people start to find their special niche, aptitude, and enthusiasms. A person turns from a late adolescent into an adult. Hopefully they find their true vocation. This is partly done through formal study, but equally through the myriad of activities which take up just as much time, from talking through games and sports to clubs and associations.

The many clubs and societies are funnels or doorways into new ways which may absorb a person's emotions and thoughts for a whole life, for example drama, law, politics, the church, business, music or many other vocations. It is where a person can discover at a serious level what their real interests are and make the first important contacts with an outside, grown-up, world which will encourage them in these interests. Most vocational commitments require both enthusiasm and aptitude. At University you can discover if you have these.

Universities from their start did something of this, channelling people into the Church, Law, Politics, Education and so on. But now, with the huge proliferation of possibilities for a creative life, a student at Oxford I entered a kind of chamber with many doors leading off it, with headings like 'Drama,' 'Philanthropy,' 'Travel,' and 'Art' over them. I could try several of the rooms and if I was a success begin to become an expert, make useful contacts, and then pursue this enthusiasm through my life.

This funnelling activity, alongside the many life skills which are enjoyably learnt by working with people in a club or society

– how to run things, how to work with people, how to enthuse and be enthused – partly explains the proliferation of clubs and societies.

* * *

There is quite a bit in the school reports on my artistic progress, and I wrote several essays on painting, architecture, the renaissance and other such topics. In my visit to the Louvre on the French tour I commented candidly on the fact that I felt that, compared to music or poetry, I was artistically dead. I have some of my paintings, and I have enough to show that this is not absolutely so. But I did realize that whereas music and poetry could give me a sense of ecstasy and lead me into other realms, painting and buildings could please but not amaze.

So I shall here devote some attention to my musical development. I don't remember learning to play an instrument at the Dragon, though I have dwelt on the delights of Gilbert and Sullivan. At some point I procured a mouth organ and later a guitar. I continued to sing at Sedbergh, both in quartets (though this was called off according to my letters) and in larger choirs. I sang in the *Messiah* and it may have been here that I first encountered the composer who would mean more to me than all others – Handel. I also sang in Haydn's *Creation*. So I enjoyed singing, though I was not particularly good at it. Singing, however, required that one learnt to sight-read, and I did learn a rough approximation of this skill, though I was too lazy to really become good at it.

As regards playing an instrument, I seem to remember some piano lessons at some stage, but I showed no gift or enthusiasm for this. What I did become extremely enthusiastic about was the guitar. My letters and accounts give a sense of my enthusiasm, especially after I discovered the pleasures of playing in a 'skiffle' group. Here with washboard and tea chest double bass, I performed my first concerts to my (if not others) delight. This was when I learnt the joys of not only Lonnie Donegan and other skiffle, but also blues music (I learnt to play some blues and talk of Big Bill Broonzy, and remember going wild over Christ Barber and others), and also pop music. I mention going to the films of Elvis Presley and give quite an amusing account of how ridiculous he looked, but how wonderful the music was. So I entered the joy of making music with others, but also of impersonating Elvis and my other great favourite, Buddy Holly. My parents' obvious enthusiasm for this pop music, which they and my sisters and friends sung along to gamely, added to the pleasure.

My uncle Richard was learning the clarinet at this time and my holidays were penetrated by the sound of his efforts, in particular Mozart's haunting clarinet concerto. I used to argue fiercely with Richard about whether pop music was better than classical. I remember him playing me pop classics when I was first at Sedbergh and they meant nothing to me. In that strange way that suddenly one discovers as one grows up a new pleasure, like adult foods or books, I suddenly began to enjoy classical music when I was fifteen or sixteen.

I had a tape recorder and began to be able to record my own music – much better than the scratchy 78 vinyl gramophone we bought when I was about 15 and its two first records, including 'Red Sails in the Sunset.' On the tape recorder I remember recording Bach's 'Coffee Cantata' which became a favourite

– influenced I think by my mother. I also liked Beethoven. But it was really only when I went to Oxford and went live classical music, that I found a real passion for listening to music.

* * *

The fourth area was a training in what might roughly be called 'hobbies and interests.' Much of my time from about the age of nine up to university was spent in playing with various levels of 'toys' or tools. This enthusiasm for hobbies is a very marked feature of British life, a peculiarity noted by my friends from other cultures such as Japan, and by some perceptive British writers themselves. For example George Orwell drew attention to another English characteristic which is so much a part of us that we barely notice it, and that is the addiction to hobbies and spare time occupations, the privateness of English life.' He continued 'We are a nation of flower-lovers, but also a nation of stamp-collectors, pigeon-fanciers, amateur carpenters, coupon-snippers, darts-players, cross-world-puzzle fans.'[1] These passions developed in my life from about the age of six.

At the Dragon School stage many of my hobbies revolved around of small models of reality – cars, soldiers, animals, construction kits like meccano and minibricks. At the school these were supplemented by various passions, crazes as we called them, when everyone would start to collect or swop certain items, or build little objects. At Sedbergh I turned from small-scale models to other hobbies, most important of all being fishing, but also playing my guitar. At university the skills learnt

---

1 GEORGE ORWELL, *The Lion and the Unicorn,* 1941, p. 39.

here were continued but then channelled increasingly into adult activities, in particular academic work. Some of these hobbies and passions were individual occupations, but many were again shared with friends and formed the basis for some of our deepest friendships.

It is difficult to capture the multi-level pleasure of these hobbies which could occupy much of one's waking thought and emotion, but here is a very brief sketch of the most important in my life between the age of about twelve and the end of university.

Fishing for 'game' fish was encouraged particularly at Sedbergh, where I did the bulk of my fishing, and by the fact that I lived in the excellent trout fishing Lake District from the age of twelve. Without going into any detail about the content of the fishing, here are a few ways in which I think fishing shaped me, as did all our private hobbies and passions, which were encouraged by our schools.

Throughout my life, fishing was a justified escape. It was a licence to be alone and in control of one's own thoughts and destiny. It was a calming, zen-like, pursuit and I early discovered that it took me away into my own world. It was also a craft or art, a path or special calling, the kind of special skill which is termed a way (Dao, Tao or Do) in Chinese and Japanese, as in Ju-do, Ken-do, Cha-do.

I think that fishing must have meant so much because it focuses several things together. The escape to loneliness, something akin to what Yeats describes in his poem on 'An Irish Airman Foresees his Death' or St Exupery memorably captures in *Flight to Arras*. A time to think and sort out in a quiet way the pressures of growing up. Then there is clearly the excitement.

Everything is still and in waiting, then the sudden tug, splash, flash of gold beneath the water and the battle is on. Then there was the fact that it took one to so many beautiful places. I would never have spent hours at dawn, in the heat of the day, at sunset and even at night in glorious countryside, watching the changing seasons, noting the minutiae of insect and other life, and entranced by swiftly flowing water which soothes the eyes, if I had not fished.

Then there was the praise and esteem of others – a special treat to cook, eat and perhaps share one's trout in a school where food was short. Then the sociability, the discussions, the stories told, and especially the sharing with my father who I found it more difficult to relate to as I grew older and more immersed in intellectual things

Finally it was an outlet for my dreams and plans. I would spend the barren winters drawing maps, making flies, repairing rods, working out stratagems. Then through the summer in numerous different streams, lochs and tarns I would pit myself against the foe. The passion was greatest precisely in these five years before going on to Oxford. It took over from electric trains, airguns, toy soldiers and other hobbies and was what I dreamt about, talked about and became most excited about. Later it ebbed over the years.

* * *

It looks as if there is parallel between the four stages I have outlined and the types of imaginative play in my life. A first glance at the way I played during my first five years in India shows that I was a little Hunter Gatherer. I fished and learnt to swim; I climbed trees and balanced on swings; I explored streams and woods; I carried things in barrows, prams and small toy cars. So my play seems to be mainly about external activities. There are no signs in the photographs of the time of models, construction kits, toy soldiers or animals.

This phase of external playing went on for a year or a little more when I returned to England at the age of five and a quarter. Probably it started to change when I started to go to my first school when I was six. Early photographs on my return show me again with little cars, fishing and swimming as I did in India.

Much of this activity, both in India and in my first year home was rather solitary, perhaps with one other person at most. There were no groups or gangs, no pets, no collecting and building up collections. I was just roaming around and experimenting. There were no organised team games, though there is one photograph of me playing cricket with one other person. I was on my own, learning to forage and be a hunter-gatherer.

From about the age of seven or eight I changed into a group animal, a collector and acquirer of property, and a builder up of things. I had property, I joined gangs, I delighted in building up empires of small models – cars, planes, animals, minibricks etc. So in what was now childhood, rather than infancy, I was working out how to organise my life in miniature, in a ratio in my models of about 1:100 – in other words my trains or animals were about one hundredth life size.

Again this phase of models and fairy stories and so on did not immediately change when I moved on to my next, public school and our home in northern England. I still had my trains and soldiers and read imaginative books. But around puberty, in other words around the age of 14 to 15, I moved into a new play and imagination phase. This I describe in my books on that stage as one of deeper friendship and group activity, and a series of activities which were now at the scale of 1: 2 with adulthood, half-size. The team games, the learning to play rock and skiffle roll on my guitar, learning to ride a motorbike, a passion for trout fishing, and my first tentative love affairs from about 17. In this period I was simulating adulthood both in my play, but also in my school work which was increasingly concerned with adult themes – serious politics, economics, social affairs and religion. This is the period when my childhood 'enchantment' started to ebb and I found myself in the in-between land between my child's world and the adult one ahead.

Once again there was a lag in the next change. The first year at Oxford seems to have been the end of adolescence, there was an enchanted first love affair in my first summer filled with fantasies, the symbol was the Lord of the Rings and C. S. Lewis and T. H. White's 'Once and Future King' which I was reading and trying to act out. This was the period of Keats and Wordsworth and the romantic attempt to hold on to an undivided world, a last struggle to hold on to my religious faith as a Protestant Christian. Then the work became more involving, the affairs with girls became more intense and intellectual and the team games faded away. I became really involved in the imaginative reconstruction that is proper history. So my work became my play, and my play became my work.

FOUR

Head and Heart

WE WERE SENT to school, so our parents told us, to 'be educated,' which for many has the meaning of sitting in classes and learning things. We were to learn mental skills, both the content and ways of thought. The aim was to train me to think well, to develop my brain in a way which would make me a competent member of whatever profession I later chose. The training was both in content and form.

The content are linguistic ability, particularly important in foreign lands, skill in writing and expressing oneself clearly and arithmetic. Also I was to have knowledge of history, geography, the classics of literature, and a dash of science. This was to give us the tools of thought and expression, to be able to argue, persuade, solve problems, generally lead confidently.

The training was rather general for it was to prepare a foundation for the training of doctors, administrators, lawyers, managers, academics and anyone whose job it is to take a tough knot of complex issues, unravel them, and then put forward a viable solution – usually choosing the lesser of two evils. Yet while we should work hard and be keen on the development of the intellect, we should not be arrogant if we were successful, we should not be over-brainy, too obsessive. It should all be achieved as effortlessly (apparently) as possible.

How this was in fact practised over the fifteen years of my life between six and twenty-one, is not easy to summarize. But looking at the whole process several things stand out.

One is that what I went through was an integrated, directed and purposeful system where the final desired outcome was present from the start. The Dragon School was in North Oxford and many of the teachers had been either at Oxford or Cambridge. At Sedbergh School, though it seemed remote, all but one master in the school had been through Oxbridge (and the exception was the French master who had been to a French university). In other words, all of them had been through a similar system to the one in which they were now teaching, including the stages of preparatory and public schools.

So, from the first day at the Dragon I was being prepared, if I was up to the standard, for Oxbridge. What then would I need in terms of mental tools to end up, for example, at Christchurch, Oxford, where we used to go once a year from the Dragon School for a service?

I would need to have a good memory. The constant examinations, often termly and certainly every year up to University were always partly tests of memory. No books or notes could be taken into the exams and all our arguments had to be backed up by 'facts.' So we were encouraged to learn the basics by heart, internalize the rules and structures, whether in Latin, English, Mathematics or History. 'Rote learning,' for example of the dates of the King's of England, the tenses of a Latin verb, or a piece of poetry, were however known to be fairly mechanical skills. While they were a foundation, they were no more than that. It was what was built on them that was important.

Other, more refined skills, were essential. One was taste and discrimination. We were presented with numerous arguments, approaches, opinions, views on all sorts of matters, from history to biology, and we had to learn how to judge between them, to decide that this was a better argument, this was a more beautiful poem or painting, that this piece of evidence was true or false, that this fact was of core importance or just a superficial oddity. So we should learn to weigh, investigate, test, use various comparative and logical methods to come up with 'the truth,' or as accurate a picture as we could obtain of it.

Once we had come up with a convincing conclusion, we had to learn how to persuade others to accept our interpretation. In other words, we had to learn the arts of presentation, rhetoric, of enticement and entertainment, of logical progress and surprising twist.

Obviously we had to learn the content in a range of basic subjects. At my first kindergarten aged five I was doing Recitation, Reading, Writing, Mathematics and Tables. By the end of my primary school, aged eight and a half, I was doing Reading, Writing, Spelling, Composition, History, Scripture, Arithmetic, Algebra, Nature Study, Geography, Handiwork, Art, Physical Training, Games.

Throughout most of my time at the Dragon School, between the age of eight and 13, I was doing Latin, English, Mathematics, French, Geography, Divinity and Science, as well as handicrafts, art and games.

Looking back I am surprised at the relatively high level and breadth of what we were expected to know at the time.

* * *

This fairly broad education, which narrowed after about the age of 15 and the 'Ordinary' or 'O' level exams as we decided to specialize in arts, sciences or language, was based on a particular type of teaching.

From about eight years old to ten we sat at our desks and the teachers fed us with 'facts' and set us exercises to test our basic knowledge of the elementary features of the main subjects. But even then they encouraged us to ask questions and to challenge them if we disagreed with something they said. By the end of those five years at the Dragon, we were already partly independent thinkers, working out things for ourselves in a mildly creative way.

This pattern was repeated at public school. From 13 to 15 we repeated the earliest pattern, but at a higher level, that is the learning of facts, keeping to our desks and passing of standardized exams. Then in the last three years, and particularly the last two in the upper sixth form as it was called, we moved into what I now recognize as a quasi-university style teaching. We only occasionally sat listening to our teachers summarizing material and learning things by heart. Normally we were set essays on diverse subjects, given suggested readings, then told to go off and do research in the library and come back with as polished and convincing an essay as possible. Then the essay would be read and comments and marks assigned (with the Greek form of marking, from alpha to gamma which was used at University). And we might go for a 'tutorial' to the master's house, alone or with a fellow pupil, to discuss our work at more length.

What was happening now was that our teachers were becoming mentors, teaching us how to improve through encouragement and suggestions for improvement. They praised us, exhorted us, and showed us our weaknesses. We admired them and wanted to delight and please them, so we tried hard. The carrot became more important than the stick.

* * *

Oxford took all of this one stage further. The first year was a replay of sixth form – some exams, learning facts and new skills, sticking to the texts and the books we were told to read. But in the second and particularly the last year we were expected to take off. We were expected to find out new things, make new arguments or construct unexpected, ingenious, creative solutions to the problems we were set in a way which would delight our teachers and surprise our friends. It was by now not what you knew, for you were expected to have the framework of facts, but how deeply you had thought about the subject, how you expressed your argument, how ambitious and innovative you were.

At first my hard work continued as at school under pressure from my teachers, who expected me to produce written work every few days or a week or so. Later the drive came from within as my curiosity, interest and desire to please my teachers increased. And the hard work was not just in the short eight week terms, for we were expected to do quite a bit of reading and preparation during the Vacations, and even to write one or two essays.

My second year, 1961–2, was also crucial in terms of organizing my work. It is when I really professionalized my work and above all my archiving. The five by three inch cards became frequent; I started to keep carbon copies of significant letters, I learnt to touch type from a Pitman's course and bought a typewriter, and my notes started to be typed. I was now keeping all my mother's letters and most of my ephemera and all my work. I was also writing much more in the way of occasional pieces, especially poetry. So it was really from about the age of twenty that the 'total archiving' was born.

Left to plan my own intellectual life, I learnt to cram in an enormous amount in a day, reading, writing, social and love life, entertainment and sport. It was at Oxford that I really learnt time management and above all the ability to switch from one task to another and give each one total concentration.

There was a great disconnect between my academic work – which was intense and quite high level – and the kind of sentimental poetry, letters to friends and other writing. I had learnt the art of 'changing gears' in communication.

* * *

While I remember the Oxford undergraduate years as a sort of romantic paradise, in fact, my papers show much more of the depression, conflict, stress and strain (particularly through work) of the time. It was both wonderful and difficult. In fact, what memory has mostly erased was the immense work effort of those three years and how far I had become immersed in history and political science.

By the end of undergraduate life you were ready for any profession within your general field of arts or sciences. You then went on to a more specific training for a particular profession. In my case this was to be a teacher, specifically a teacher at the tertiary or university level. So I undertook the apprenticeship of doing a doctorate in history, a D.Phil., the qualification which just at that time was becoming the necessary one for going on to be a teaching academic.

If I had decided after my undergraduate life to go into another profession, a civil servant, lawyer, clergyman, businessman, aid worker, the first few years after graduating would have been an intellectual apprenticeship of a not dissimilar kind. I would have been apprenticed to a 'supervisor' in that profession, whether in a set of legal chambers, in a hospital, in a theological college, where I would have learnt the particular sub-set of skills for that profession.

In other words, what my education to the end of my undergraduate years did was to lay a generic groundwork upon which my profession could be built. Aged 21 I had the tools which could be applied to a wide range of what we now call 'white collar' jobs, in other words professional jobs which we characteristically do not with our bodies, as with 'blue collar' jobs, but where we use our minds, expressing ourselves through talking and writing.

By combining the character side of the education, which taught the personality and interpersonal skills, with the intellectual side, we were supposed to be in a position where, with some luck and perhaps using some of the contacts created by our education, we could enter into any profession and be reasonably successful.

Above all I was taught to be hopeful and ambitious, to strive for the highest. We were not to be content to be 'pen-pushers', 'jobsworthies', 'subalterns'. In the army we should end up as Generals or at least full Colonels, not Majors; we should be

Judges, not just Solicitors; we should be full Oxbridge Professors, not just Lecturers; we should be the Senior Registrars or heads of hospitals, not just doctors; CEOs of large trading firms or banks, Bishops and not just Vicars. When such 'high flyers,' as we called them, visited our schools and universities and remembered their days there in their speeches and sermons, a stellar career was placed before our imagination.

Heart and Emotion

Education is much more than just mental development. It also requires training of other parts of the human personality. One of these is the education of the heart, that is feelings towards others and oneself. This again started strongly in infancy in India in attachments to my close family and a few of those who looked after me, including Indian ayahs. It then developed into my real friendships outside the family at the Dragon School and serious, sustained, friendships from about the age of sixteen at Sedbergh. From a couple of years later I was starting to seek romantic love with girls and there were a few adolescent crushes while still at school. But the real break occurred at Oxford where my first two girl friends pre-occupied me and I began to direct my strongest feelings towards people who had started as strangers. Oxford was above all an education in the art of love, sympathy, involvement with the other, with the sexual urge controlled but always strongly present. Let me examine this a little more fully.

* * *

The central characteristic of English education is the separation of the individual from the family, so that relations with parents become in a sense contractual rather than status-based. Consequently we may wonder what replaces or fills this family-shaped hole in our affections.

'Patron' is the wrong word to describe the Master-Pupil, Master-Apprentice kind of relationship which I repeatedly went through. The Master whether in games or form, house or head master, instructed and supervised us, sharpened our skills and controlled us. But he (or she) was not a patron. After I left each stage of my education I immediately lost contact with almost all my teachers. I did keep in touch with one or two of my masters at sixth form and my teachers at University. But having performed their task of pushing me on to the next level of my education, I did not remain in any kind of permanent 'patron-client' relation with them. We later became friends.

The nearest to 'patrons' were my two doctoral supervisors, in the sense that they had trained me specifically through academic apprenticeship in the higher skills of becoming a university teacher. So they could vouch for my ability and continued to write letters in my support when I applied for jobs or promotion for some years. In return I treated them with some deference, tried to make their ideas better known, sent them copies of things I had written. But it is a very weak form of patronage, if patronage at all.

In essence, then, because I had so many different Masters (and Mistresses earlier on), perhaps 20 or more who were important in my education, I was never dependent on any particular one of them, even though letters from a house or head master or university tutor would be crucial in moving me on to the next level. I benefited from a raft of support which replaced the normal support of a father or uncle. My father, grandfather, uncles and others could give me advice, but little practical support (apart from financial and social in my education). I was to achieve success through my own exertions, even if I followed a family tradition.

Much of my education was also about that most important of arts in a situation where we cannot depend on our relatives, that is becoming close and learning to work with and trust strangers, namely the art of friendship and 'fellowship.'

From what I have already written on games, hobbies, shared studies, it is clear that a great deal of the skill I was learning was how to make (and break) friendships. I was learning how to initiate, feed, maintain, enjoy and grow increasingly trusting, shared, social relations with people who started as complete and unrelated strangers. This happened from about the age of six. But it was from about the age of ten, at the Dragon School, that I started to have proper friends, some of whom I am still in touch with.

Yet it was really from about the age of sixteen at Sedbergh School that potential life-long friendships, based on shared interest and some overlap of character started. Two or three special friends became close and we shared parts of our holidays and with one I went toured the continent in my seventeenth year. We discussed the deeper problems of life, as we saw them, and something of our characters interpenetrated each other.

This learning of the art of friendship continued at University, but part of its force was then diverted towards something else, that is friendship and mixed with it, love, for girls.

In fact through my life I have had many friendships (without romantic love) with girls, starting with my younger sisters. I found it easy to distinguish friendship from love. So by about eighteen and learning school I had girls as well as boys as friends.

Throughout these years I laid the foundations for making friends, by definition equal and non-exploitative or utilitarian. This is a skill and a pleasure which has underpinned much of my later life. The whole idea of Fellowship at Cambridge, that is 'collegiality' and working with others in teaching departments, or with my graduate students, many of whom became life-long friends, is putting into practice the art of friendship which is at the heart of living with strangers and which I learnt at school.

In sum, I was to learn to be filled with good emotions. Good emotions included things like self-confidence, cheerfulness, overcoming loneliness, the art of attracting people to one's personality, and of being attracted by them, the arts of love, hate, detachment and attachment. This is a complex web and particularly difficult because the natural place to develop these emotions, the family, was largely replaced for boarders in an artificially generated setting, the new 'quasi-family' of the school. Something which was constructed and non-familistic had to take on some of the warmth and intensity of the blood family.

* * *

The other dimension is finding that special friend, the one who is united not just by shared interest, humour, need, experience, hobbies and likes, but also through body and spirit, that bundle which we call 'love.' And here we move into one of the most important parts of my education, learnt in the classroom and playground and in the holidays, namely learning to replace the love of my family, and especially maternal love by love for someone who is initially a stranger who I had chosen for myself, romantic love.

A strong theme throughout my Dragon, Sedbergh and Oxford days is love. Elsewhere I attempt to explain a little about my search for divine love – ultimately unsuccessful. The striving for that love was not entirely distinct from human love. The two were interfused in some of my favourite poets of the time, John Donne, George Herbert, William Wordsworth and Gerard Manley Hopkins. All was part of a wider search for reciprocated love, the finding of a true soul mate.

I suppose that everyone searches for love. The love that often surrounds us in our infancy ebbs away and we try to find a replacement. This is a theme for William Wordsworth, whose mother died when he was eight and father a couple of years later, and who found a surrogate mother in Anne Tyson in Hawkshead (where I lived as a boy). It was something which was also very important for me for not entirely different reasons – my mother leaving me again and again from the age of under seven to go to India.

It has long struck me as an anthropologist that something about the social structure and socialization patterns of England has made romantic love particularly important. As I have written in several places, including half the book *Marriage and Love in England*, there is some powerful need for something to be present which 'defects of loneliness controls,' as John Donne puts it.

This general condition, the urgency to find love, was brought to particular intensity in my life by a combination of two things. Firstly the personality and needs of my mother – an intensely loving, yet in some ways damaged, person, who poured love upon my father, me, my sisters, animals, and anyone else within reach. So, for a few years, until I was nearly seven, I had enough love surrounding me. Then, as it seemed, it was suddenly withdrawn to a great distance when she went to India.

Although I knew that she still loved me, and my grandparents gave me great love and attention, I still felt that sudden loneliness, the absence of the other as described in the preface. This was obviously exacerbated when I went to boarding schools for ten years where I was away from all family love and among strangers.

I found myself a single transacting individual in a moral market economy, on my own, having to fight my own battles. My mother recognized that this was both necessary but painful. The solution was to find a love as strong as that infant love of my mother, but transformed into an equal and mature love.

At first there were hints of a reciprocated love in crushes on other little boys at the Dragon School and on bigger or smaller boys at Sedbergh. This had something of the feeling of the total, overwhelming, 'stars in the eyes' emotion. Yet, in the end, it was only a partial solution to the emptiness, of feeling of being incomplete – as were the increasing number of really deep friendships I began to form.

In the absence of a permanent and multi-level relationship of a physical, social, spiritual and 'total' kind, impossible, as I saw it, before or outside marriage, for a while the solution to the emptiness was to dream and plan for the final discovery of 'the other one.' Between the ages of about 14 and 25 I pursued my love in an idealized way, somewhat in the ancient western tradition of courtly love, where the ideal love was always unattainable.

How then did I learn what romantic love was supposed to be and how I was to express my feelings, and recognize them in others?

I certainly don't remember any direct formal school teaching on matters of the heart. We did not get talks or lectures or any form of counselling. Even 'sex education' as it is now termed was more or less totally absent. The only area where sex and love were touched on was under 'religion', in divinity lessons and sermons.

Yet, indirectly, we were constantly being shown models of how to think, feel and behave in relation to romantic love.

My growing feelings of needing a loved one, and interest in learning the craft of love, gave special resonance to many of the things I read, whether some of the great moments in William Shakespeare, the Romantic Poets (especially Keats, Shelley, Coleridge and Wordsworth), Tennyson and Swinburne, W.B. Yeats, the story of Heloise and Abelard and various great novels about love, especially Jane Austen and the Bronte sisters. The major theme of much painting was also the representation of love. A large area was my more serious reading at school, including poetry, plays, essays, the Bible and other suggested books. This was particularly important given my interest in literature (where I won the sixth form literature prize in my last term).

As well as what we learnt in class, there were many films and plays, often romantic comedies. There were comics, magazines and newspapers, much concerned with love. There were pop idols such as the new sensation Elvis Presley and much other popular music (almost all about love), and increasingly from Sedbergh days, television programs. All these would have given us clues as to what was love – and perhaps particularly advertisements where much is potentially made desirable by playing the love and romance card.

Actual people, especially my parents (a very strong model) and my grandparents, uncles and aunts, set up standards and models of what companionate love was like.

What is perhaps strange is that having experienced a shock of an early loss of the object of my love with my mother's departure, and the repeated shocks of her subsequent departures every few years just as I was building up love and trust again, I somehow remained hopeful, trusting, searching, and quite confident that 'Some day my princess would come.' As with other parts of my life I felt that if I worked hard enough, waited, applied my mind and spirit, I would one day find the person who would fill that emotional gap.

Throughout these years from puberty, as strong as any growth of the physical body, imagination, intellect and character, is my constant search for deep love – mixed up for a long time with sexual urges. Many of my most intense memories through the years are to do with encounters with potential partners.

FIVE

Spirit and Character

THE GROWTH OF an interest in spiritual matters, an intersection of what is called religion and imagination, was one of the central features of my education. In terms of ritual, we started each day throughout my ten years of schooling with a prayer and often with a reading and a hymn. We framed the day within the Christian faith and perhaps ended it on our knees in prayer. We went to a service with a sermon and prayers every Sunday. We studied 'divinity' in at least one class a week throughout the ten years.

In my case I had a particularly strong indoctrination into religion because my mother's brother was very devout and an 'Officer' at some Christian University-based, boys' camps. In half a dozen holidays from the age of about ten to my early 20s, I would go for a week or two to such camps where alongside games and expeditions we learnt more about Jesus.

And in the midst of this process, the central point just after puberty, we made a re-affirmation of our Christian membership in a special service called 'Confirmation.' This was attended by our parents or their proxies if they could not come. At this point, the only real formal ritual celebrating the change from child to adult, we became adults in religion and could henceforth commune directly with God through the drinking of Christ's blood and eating of his flesh at Holy Communion.

In terms of the growth of my ethical or moral ideas, a central theme was the tension between the growth of sexual desire at puberty, and the Christian ethic which placed celibacy above all other sexual states and strictly forbade any sexual activity outside marriage. This was a particular problem in a single-sex boys' boarding school. The strange feature of celibacy and monasticism, and the idea of pollution and the sinful body was a central feature of the kind of Christianity we were bathed in. The whole battle between lust and God was central to my growing up and part of what lay behind the idealized pursuit of romantic love.

There were other ethical difficulties. How could we reconcile 'turning the other cheek' with the schoolboy necessity to stand up to bullies? How could we love Christ before all others when we needed others much more than Him? We should always tell the truth, the ethic told us, but we knew that if we did so, either in our social relations, or when quizzed by a Master about the doings of our friends, it would be disastrous. We were told never to be greedy, but often exhausted after cold games we were exactly that. We were told to be humble and never boast, yet we were expected by the school to project our successes on the field or elsewhere so that others would be impressed and emulate us. So the ethical upbringing was filled with contradictions. We had to pick our ways through a minefield in the pursuit of our mission to both be a gentleman and a Christian.

One unusual feature was that basically, ethics were taught at school more rather than in the home. Furthermore, unlike Confucianism, we were brought up to hold that our central relationship to another human-like entity was not to our father or mother, but to a generalized God and Jesus. It was a faith which took us right out of family relations.

It was also a forward-looking, salvation-based, redemptive religion. It was based on the concept of original sin, the universal Fall after the expulsion from Eden. There was nothing about family ethics, no ancestor worship, no stress on the family at all.

So there was a launching out, in our religion, into a personalized, internalized, non-familistic, system, where we were alone with our God. It had no overlap with the family, our parents did not mediate our relationship to God, and no priest did so in this reformed Protestant religion. So the religion was deeply dissolvent of any family ritual. And likewise as I recall, apart from my uncle Richard, and going to church on Sundays with my mother when she was home and my grandparents, there was no re-enforcing of religion in our family. We did not discuss the matter and there were no family prayers or graces.

The only time religion intruded was in annual rituals (Easter and Christmas) and family rites of passage, baptism, marriage and funerals. The Christian calendar did affect us through the periodic marking of the year, Advent, Christmas, Lent, Easter, Harvest Festival. But apart from this it did not impinge very much on our family life.

* * *

At the Dragon School and in Dorset I went to Church and even studied a little divinity. I don't remember that I absorbed very much or was particularly interested.

I think several things made me seriously interested in religion at Sedbergh and as an undergraduate at Oxford. One was the influence of my uncle Richard, a devout evangelical Christian. My parents were happy (and relieved, since our holidays were always a slight problem) arranged for me to go to the Christian camp at Iwerne on some of the holidays from Sedbergh.

At Iwerne the religious instruction seeped into me. The catchy little hymns, the shining faith and kindness of the Oxbridge 'Officers,' the spirit of enthusiastic goodwill, the very muscular Christianity of it all. I learnt the techniques of prayer and bible reading.

Despite all the encouragement, however, I never had any real mystical experiences and felt frustrated that I never felt that Christ 'entered my heart.' I was told that He would become a personal friend, as others reported had happened to them, but I never felt Him close to me.

The second influence was a variant of Wordsworthian pantheism. As I walked, climbed, swam and skated in Wordsworth's childhood valley, I felt those heightened states of emotion and something of the numinous, the greater forces rolling through the rocks and stones and trees. I saw the strange lights on the mountains and felt powers which lifted me out of myself. So it was here, and in poetry, that I came closer to some kind of feeling of a supernatural force. Yet it all seemed a long way from the rather dry, practical, rational Christianity that was taught to me in my religious instruction as an Anglican.

Another influence was my mother. She was always a seeker after some ultimate solution, some truth in poetry, in Hinduism, Buddhism, Christianity, philosophy or poetry, which would answer the deeper questions. Like me she felt the closest to spiritual power in poetry and nature.

What I did find attractive in religion was that at least it attempted to give me answers to the great 'why' questions a child asks. Why are we here? Where do we go after death? Why should we be good? Why is there suffering? I remember having discussions about these subjects with some of my friends, especially at Sedbergh and Oxford. Even if the answers were mildly unsatisfactory, Christianity was a start.

Religion, I thought, seemed to be a way of creating meaning and preserving the integrity of life, stopping the disenchantment. I was not aware that one of the very deepest assaults on magic, faery, another world of spirit, was Protestant Christianity which had sent God a million miles away and attacked all miracles, magic and the interfused world of Catholicism. At that time I somehow felt that at least religion tied things together, it supplied a morality that was relevant to political, economic and social life, it seeped through the strengthening borders that increasingly split my life into parts.

* * *

In some ways my Sedbergh years could be seen as a struggle between my mind, heart and body, or between sex, religion and intellect. This continued in Oxford. I arrived very devout and remained active in Christian circles through my undergraduate years – going to St Aldate's, going on several OICCU camps in Dorset and a retreat in Devon. I also attended the College Chapel and formed a close friendship with Alec Graham, chaplain and a future Bishop. We went on a walking holiday together and to two Borstal camps. He fell into the category of an older mentor, but more on the spiritual side and I remember confessing my sexual frustration to him and his being very wise and understanding. So I tried to force myself to be Christian – and was even vaguely teetotal and remember sitting in priggish mute criticism when my parents drove to Scotland and stopped off for a drink at a hotel.

Yet, as the years progressed, I felt increasingly uneasy about my Christian beliefs. It was partly the old question – why had god allowed so much suffering (at this time the Bangladesh war and famine) and pain. Lewis's 'Problem of Pain' did not satisfy and his 'Screwtape Letters' amused but did not altogether halt the doubts.

The turning point, I think, must have been when I was about 21. I remember reading my first anthropology book, the BBC lectures on 'The Institutions of Primitive Society.' I began to have a relativist outlook and to wonder what Christians made of the heathen. No doubt all of this was fanned by my mother. Her liberation from Christianity and from western superiority occurred around the same time. Anyway, I remember questioning the authorities at the boys' camp and getting a rather testy answer – and knowing I could not go on. The door was shut.

I have often wondered whether comparative anthropology both undermined my beliefs – already shaken under the assault of Gibbon, Voltaire, Tocqueville and others, but at the same time helped to fill the vacuum left by such an undermining of a framework from my youth.

Anthropology provided a way to understand the world around me. It answered the why as well as the how questions. It gave a richness and mystery to life, but without dogmatism or privileging one religion. I read one of the favourite books of my mother, *The Perennial Philosophy* by Aldous Huxley, and other modern philosophical works. My mother gave me the Bhagavad Gita – though I did not make much of it.

The wider interests of that flower-power generation – the Beatles, and Buddhist thought started to make Protestant England seem rather small and provincial.

So I became enamoured of anthropology and world religion, and at last abandoned the belief which had never really satisfied or brought the 'Light of the World' into my heart. I felt, alongside many other liberations, a lightness of being to realize that I did not need this crutch. That I could think for myself, challenge, not need to accept authority or assertions that where were some mysteries too deep to understand.

* * *

Another way of considering the matter is to look at the development of an area which we might call spiritual imagination. That is the forming of habits connected with the development of my cultural and creative life. This covers a very range of activities and thoughts. It started strongly, as I have documented as a child and at the Dragon, in a rich imaginative life of children's activities. There were games, fantasies, 'let's pretend' virtual worlds, the investing of my toys and activities with a reality just as strong as other parts of my life. The films, pantomimes, stories and other artistic experiences blended with my creative games-playing with family and friends to produce a thriving alternative world.

At Sedbergh this transformed itself, though it never died. Now it was an imaginative exploration through new books, romantic poetry, films, music, fishing, boating, and many activities which were again invested with wider meanings. All this was an education in cultural and imaginative skills which included the use of language, appreciation of the arts, and in particular the joys of living in the beautiful valley where Wordsworth had been a boy and the glorious hills around Sedbergh.

This imaginative transformation from childhood to adult imagination and cultural creation was continued at Oxford. In many ways the richest part of my Oxford experience was the expansion of my spirit through new encounters with music, drama, films, books and especially poetry. I increasingly tried to create as well as absorb meaning through starting to write prose and poetry in order to express my heightened sense of the stimulating life I was experiencing.

Also important was the education of the spirit. That is the growing search for meaning, for truth, for ethical imperatives, for understanding, coherence and pattern in a jumble of events and feelings. This verges on what in the west is taken to be the religious sphere. This was not consciously something that I thought much about until I went to Sedbergh. As a child and at the Dragon I had conformed without much analysis of what I was doing. I had assumed that there was a God and that the world was basically subject to His laws. Things happened for a purpose, there was life after death and that there was a spiritual dimension to everything. The evangelical boys' camps I went to from around the age of eleven were mainly fun-filled occasions and Christ knocking on my heart's door was largely a background figure.

It was around the time that I was confirmed that I began to become concerned with the 'meaning of life' questions. From then until the end of my undergraduate years the same quest we find in the people I admired, particularly the great poets and novelists, especially Wordsworth, Keats Yeats, Gerard Manley Hopkins, Tennyson, became central to my life. The search was for answers to the 'Why' questions – why am I here; why is there pain; why do things happen as they do; why should we be good? I tried to find assurance within conventional, evangelical Anglicanism. At Oxford I began to realise that such an easy faith was not sustainable.

What I did not realize as I went through the spiritual strife of my latter day pilgrim's progress was that my attempt to cling to childhood certainties, the wholeness and integration of childhood, was that all this was bound to be challenged at the end of school and at Oxford. Looking back now from a lifetime of anthropological and historical research into this process of the development of western civilization, I realize that the disembedding, the dissociation, the disenchantment, the splitting of head and heart, whatever one likes to call it, is both the triumph and the tragedy at the heart of what we call 'modernity.'

To become a functional individual and a rational actor in a highly mobile, individualistic, capitalist, democratic society, I had to learn to separate off my life into different spheres – economic action, political action, social action and religious belief. Yet by doing so and increasing efficiency and flexibility, I was also destroying the meanings which the overlap of these areas of our lives had created. How I overcame this process is the central theme of my life's work, but the problems were at their most acute in the last two years of undergraduate life at Oxford.

Character and Personality

Several things surprise me about what I now realize I was absorbing through these twenty-one years. One is the degree to which many of the values and goals clashed and therefore how much judgement had to be exercised. I should be strong and competitive and brave and forceful, but also not bully, not worry about being defeated by someone better, be co-operative and kind. So I was always learning how to walk tightropes, the middle way between unacceptable extremes.

Another thing that strikes me is that I was learning all these skills simultaneously, in so many ways and in so many places. A game of football taught honesty, co-operation, courage, humour, risk-assessment, logic and perhaps even rhetoric, just as much as playing marbles in the playground, taking part in a Gilbert and Sullivan opera, learning in our formal classes, or listening to sermons and lectures.

What happened at school was complemented by our home life, where we would practise and develop many of the skills – bearing pain in illness, bicycling, shooting, dealing with girls, learning friendship and how to deal with adults. So it was a complex package, where the example of others, the ethos and ethics of the institutions, the organization of different activities, the encouragement and disincentives we received, all influenced us in a multi-dimensional way.

* * *

From my time at the Dragon onwards, I was being shaped into a sort of model of the English gentleman. The Dragon or

Sedbergh was training me to be a tough, trustworthy, humorous, self-deprecating, clever, a leader of men, individualistic yet a team player, able to overcome obstacles in the most difficult situations, a survivor and a true Christian knight. Bits of these models occur in Chaucer and in Shakespeare, and through our teaching in literature we were given instruction. But much was to be instilled into us more indirectly. And against all of these models we could set the model of the bad life – the bad sport, the liar, the fanatic, the bully, the libertine, the toady, the swot, the cheat....

It was also a long process because the all-purpose, rounded, person we were training to be, with the skills to achieve in whatever profession we entered was complex. It was not just a matter of learning a particular skill – to play an instrument superbly, to be a great football player, to be a brilliant painter or a stirring orator. We had to have a modicum of all these, but a whole set of them together. We had to learn to speak, act and above all be, in our inner core, a gentleman. We had to learn to have an integrity, confidence, impartiality and tough perseverance which would preserve us as we rose to the exposed heights of whatever profession we wished to follow.

Normally such domestication and tempering is done in the household and with a much more circumscribed set of persons; a boy learns agricultural or craft or business skills from his father and uncles, a girl from her mother and aunts. But in my school system it was done through instituted machines for turning us into versatile social beings who could operate in a series of complex space.

It was clear that to succeed at almost any profession, from music to law to politics to business, one needed self-discipline, concentration and perseverance. They were especially important in a highly mobile and insecure world, and in the overseas Empire with its huge temptations, tribulations, setbacks and loneliness. So much of the education was to prepare us to be tough and ready for this.

Much of my education was about learning to use our time profitably. I had to allocate, store, share, save, use our time to achieve many different goals. Certainly this was something which struck me about the Dragon and Sedbergh – the obsession with clocks and bells. My life has been modelled round 'Time is money,' and the urban time rhythms which American sociologists have equated with urban modernity were a central feature of our training and became internalized.

* * *

An important feature of the background is the degree to which education was independent of the State. The normal situation in much of the world, for example in traditional Confucian education, is that they are identical. The educational system must not criticize and is primarily designed at the higher level to administrators. The same is true of conventional Islamic education and was increasingly over absolutist Europe from the seventeenth century. What was odd about both the schools and the Universities of Britain and later of America is their independence from the State – hence students are allowed to think for themselves, criticize (within limits) and innovate etc. An entirely different situation.

So I see a curious absence in my schooling, on the whole, of the intrusion of the nation state. Parliamentary elections had some impact, but in general there was little interference or interest in the State. Royal birthdays and particularly the Coronation of Queen Elizabeth in 1953 were to be celebrated. But there was very little in the way of flag-waving or National Anthems. I was later on interested later on in politics, and read Henry V's Agincourt speech with pride and studied other Shakespearian plays and political history. But on the whole, schooling was separated off from the State. And, being private schools, there was only very light supervision or interference at that time. Our teachers, from school to university, were not employees of the State or Civil Servants, as they are in France, Japan and many countries today.

* * *

There is also the question of how much we were already being prepared and advised ahead on our professional careers. Looking at this, it is curious how little attention was paid to any kind of careers advice. Even in my last years at Oxford, I do not remember any official advice, and none, I think was given at Sedbergh for those who were not going on to University.

The only action that was taken, and this happened from very early on at the Dragon and continued throughout our education, was to put before us various options as represented by successful examples of various professions. So at Sedbergh, for example, we were given talks by diplomats, businessmen, journalists and clergymen. etc. and any one of these might inspire us to think of a career in such a field. Throughout there were special-interest clubs, for instance in music or drama, science or making things, which might kindle an interest which would lead us to become some kind of professional.

On the whole, however, the view seemed to be that we would gravitate towards a particular profession. If we worked hard and were good at what we were doing, someone would notice us. Or we might be ushered towards an occupation which our ancestors had been associated with. If our ancestors, as in my case, were planters, clergymen and engineers on my father's side, and lawyers, army officers, academics on my mother's, there were many possibilities ahead. In the later 1950s up to the early 1970s, as I came onto the market, the economy was growing fast and professional jobs were proliferating, so it was a particularly optimistic and open period when the world lay before us.

* * *

The new identity in which I was being forged was of the single, all-purpose, all sufficient, individual, no longer primarily a son or daughter, brother or sister, but a member of wider society. The first separation from the womb, then the breaks that I have described elsewhere, all took me along a passage which went though the separateness of education but did not just change our status from child to adult. It changed us from being a member of a family, our position based on birth and status, to a member of society, our position based on negotiated 'contractual' relations with strangers.

The same process, of course, had happened to the vast majority of the population in the past through the other main mechanisms of servanthood and apprenticeship. I had not experienced these kinds of transition except in a very minor form – servanthood when I was for a year a 'fag' or servant of the senior boys at my public school, and apprenticeship to my doctoral supervisor. But all of these rites had the same disembedding function.

The difference about the upper, professional, educational route which I took was that while a servant was always ultimately in the control of another, which is the essence of servanthood – we were to be free and only controlled by our own sense of responsibility, duty and self worth.

We were also not engaged, as many servants were, particularly on farms, or apprentices to crafts and trades, in using our bodies to move material objects around. We were not trained to be mandarins, to scorn physical activities. The emphasis on games and toughness, on hobbies and making things, all ensured that we did not despise or scorn the physical world. Long finger nails or bound feet were not well adapted to playing rugger or tennis, or even making models or fly-fishing.

Nevertheless, it was principally through using our minds, then mediating our thoughts through speech and writing, that we moved matter around, by controlling other people – rather than shaping it directly with our own hands. Our main tools were symbolic, speech and writing, which are both very powerful but also take a very long training to make really powerful.

The bulk of the population, who went in the past straight out of their families into some form of servant, apprentice, labouring role, gained their living more directly by using their minds to control their own bodies which pushed, pulled, lifted, directed animals or machines, made pots or cars.

So in some ways, in the graduated learning of how to

manipulate symbols, my life has some resemblance to a Chinese Mandarin, not on in the concentration on mental skills but also in the heavy stress on moral and ethical character. But it is also very different. And this would have been even more pronounced if instead of becoming a teacher, I had become an army general, a bishop, a judge or a banker.

* * *

So we should espouse a set of broadly gentlemanly, Christian, ethics and moral standards. We should learn love, hope and charity, turning the other cheek, honesty even when no one was looking, doing 'small, unremembered acts of kindness and of love.' Our moral system should be within us and not followed because of fear or external controls. This might lead to loneliness, but we should learn to face loneliness. It might lead to lost opportunities for gain and advancement. But we should remember that our rewards were a better sense of self-worth, as well, perhaps, as in heaven. So we were being taught the deepest qualities – how to love, how to hate, what to value, what to scorn, who we were and what we should become.

I should learn how to compete fiercely, to defend myself, to fight and to conquer. I should become physically strong, yet gentle with it, not be a bully or too competitive. I should learn how to give and to receive graciously, and with gratitude. I should learn to share my good fortune with others, but also not to boast or triumph over those around me. I should learn not to envy others or feel hurt by their successes, but rather enlarged by their happiness. I should learn how to say no and how to say yes, without giving offence or causing jealousy. I should learn how to mourn my losses, to feel grief deeply, yet also to be brave and able to comfort others.

I should learn how to remember things that were important and practise the art of memory, but equally I should be able to forget – or at least lock away – what I did not need to remember. I should learn to see no evil, hear no evil and speak no evil. Yet I should also enjoy the pleasures of gossip and shared intimacies.

* * *

I should be full of hope about the future, whatever my experiences of the past. I should be filled with curiosity and delight, but also prepared for long periods of tedious and boring effort and patient waiting. So I should be dogged and persevering, yet realize when further effort was futile. I should be resilient, so that minor and even major setbacks did not destroy my will. I should strongly desire to win and conquer if I could, yet I should also be prepared to concede defeat graciously and without bitterness or self-doubt. I should be ingenious and original, yet be aware of the rules by which effort in any sphere must be guided.

I should be highly individual, self-aware and confident in my own judgement. I should keep my private counsel, not dependent on others to prop me up. Yet I should also be a good team-player, sociable, affectionate, knowing when to share and when to keep to myself. I should be solemn about serious matters, but also have a developed sense of the ridiculous, a humour which could tease and reduce tension, and acquire an ability to attack power or stupidity through irony and satire.

I should be charming when charm was needed, but also be

prepared to be stern and to say no if that was required. I should be certain of my own values and priorities, but also tolerant and understanding of others who did not share them. I should manage my time carefully so as not to waste it, yet also be able to relax, to conserve energy and re-charge myself, to forget the internal clock and to enter timelessness. Thus I should learn how to save time, and how to spend it, how to prioritize what was important, how to do several things quickly, one after the other, or even at the same time.

I should learn to appreciate beauty in all its forms – in art, poetry, music, nature, and people. Yet I should not be dismissive of the poor, the ugly, the deformed or the miserable. I should value people for themselves and not for the externals, whether of wealth, success, force of character, family background. I should acquire the art of friendship and the judging of character, and how to face the loss of friendship. I should treat people as ends and not as means, learn to separate head and heart, how to tell the truth, but also to refrain from telling the truth if it damaged others.

I should learn how to handle relationships with people who were very different from me – girls, adults, foreigners, and people from other social classes or different occupations. In these I should show generosity, courtesy without condescension, interest without prurience. I should not think of myself as either superior or inferior, but equal, though, through chance I might have more material and social advantages.

I should be able to assess the likely outcomes of my actions, the general degree of risk in any activity and whether it was worth taking a chance. I should be courageous and ready to do dangerous things, but not foolhardy to the extent that I put others or myself in unnecessary danger.

A Wider World:
Consequences and Comparisons

I took my experience of going through the British educational system in the middle of the 20th century for granted. I thought at the time that this was obviously the only way in which a reasonable educational system could work. I did not compare it with other systems or think about its consequences.

It was really only when I became an anthropologist and made many visits to India, Nepal, Japan and China that I began to see how unusual was the process whereby I was taken out of my family and placed in a wider society. And it has only been very recently, as I studied the history of my own University of Cambridge and my own life, that I have begun to see how deeply our modern world has been shaped by this unique system.

Here I want to widen out the account, firstly looking at some of the effects of the kind of education I have described, and then to set it in comparison to that in Continental Europe and the Far East. Education is the both a mirror of a civilization, and a machine for reproducing its deeper structures. It shapes our world and the British educational system has transformed and is transforming the world now and is worthy of our attention.

SIX

Some Ways in Which Education Shaped the English World

IN MY BOOK *The Invention of the Modern World*, I looked at some of the bundle of features which characterize the first 'modern' country (in my terms), namely England. It is worth re-examining these briefly in relation to the question of how a certain kind of education generated modernity.

Early in the book I looked at the nature of war, trade and empire in the history of England. England was a warlike, but also a trading nation. It was involved in constant warfare – but on others' soil, with others' troops, or at sea. It also built its wealth on trade. And from the seventeenth to nineteenth centuries it created the vast Empire upon which 'the sun never set.' But how could such a tiny island do this?

The warlike and belligerent nature of the English is clearly associated in my training in competitive games and those same games also taught us the rudiments of how to trade and compete in the market society whose blueprint had been made by the economist Adam Smith. From my playground games such as marbles and conkers, we were prepared for a later life in the commerce, trade or the army, in early days in the East India Company, nowadays in the banks and stock market. Our education was a preparation for capitalist games.

It also prepared us for our role in administering or profiting from what was becoming the largest Empire in the world. In the training for leadership, and in the toughening up to face loneliness, I an many others were being explicitly trained for leadership either within Britain, or anywhere in the world where we ventured.

The power of the Empire and the effectiveness of the naval and military machine which backed it on this small island largely came from its market capitalist economy. England had had a very sophisticated capitalist economy stretching back hundreds of years. It was full of money, markets, relatively free but skilled labour, banks, limited liability, the stock exchange, mortgages and many other devices to help move capital and labour around. It was like this for many centuries before the industrial revolution, at least from the twelfth century.

This capitalist system was based on the idea of private property and the right of the individual to keep the fruits of his or her own labour. As we have seen, Max Weber argued that capitalism is born when the social and the economy, the family and the individual, are separated and each child is 'free' to pursue his or her own social and economic goals. The educational system in England, which prizes the child away from their parents at a young age, whether they physically move or remain at home, sending them off to paid labour or schools, is a central foundation for capitalism in this sense.

The tendency of most societies is for wealth differences to turn into legal and ritual differences, what Tocqueville calls 'caste.' England is the great exception. Its peculiar statuses of aristocrat, gentleman, yeoman, labourer were found nowhere else in the world. They were part of a hierarchical, class, society which developed from Anglo-Saxon times. Meanwhile all other

Eurasian societies moved towards 'caste.' This hierarchy-with-mobility is an essential basis for modernity.

Tocqueville's observation that England had not reverted to 'caste,' that it had moved to a fluid class system with no fixed, birth-given, barriers, is central. The education system has been the major structural device in enabling such an unusual outcome. Although not a fully meritocratic system, the multiple forms of education enabled effective children to climb, or at least to have enough basic education, combined with character-enhancing qualities such as self-confidence, to rise in the system.

By the end of formal education, most men, and quite a number of women, were placed on the lower rungs of various professional or craft ladders which they could climb. There might also be snakes, as in the appropriate metaphor of the game of 'Snakes and Ladders,' down which a person could slither. But the basic principle was that there were opportunities for all, not necessarily from log cabin to White House, but something not too dissimilar. Any historian can point to many cases of people of humble origins becoming mighty, or at least being successful enough that they could educate their children to be great.

The class system, with a very large and diverse set of paid occupations, whether at the craftsman and small farmer level, the middle class or upper class professionals, was so diverse that the educational system had to be generic. It was best to concentrate on character and spirit, combined with the basics of numeracy, literacy and general knowledge. The specific skills of doctor, lawyer, clergyman or other professions would be learnt on the job. Education was a broad road and only at the later stages would people specialize and go off onto separate tracks.

One central peculiarity of England for many centuries has been the pattern of population. The age at marriage was usually very late (first marriage for women in the 17th century, for example, in the mid-20s) and up to a quarter of women never married. This led to a relatively small completed family size and consequently English population grew very slowly, except in periods like the later eighteenth century when there was a high demand for labour and people married younger.

The peculiar demography of England, related to the late age at marriage, is directly related to education. The connection has been noticed nowadays in many parts of the world where a rise in the educational opportunities for women in particular, as well as the introduction of rights for young people to keep their earnings from paid work rather than automatically giving it to their kin, has led to a dramatic fall in family size. In essence, the sending away of children and their separate rights cuts the tie between production and reproduction. By shedding their children, families no longer benefitted from high fertility. Parents did not benefit form their children's labour, nor could they count on their children to protect them in later life, either in crises or in old age. Children became a net cost, for their childhood and education, and not a benefit.

Since it can be argued that it was the slow rise of population over the period from the later middle ages, which did not absorb the steady economic growth over those centuries, which provided the essential capital for the agricultural and industrial revolutions, the separation of the productive and reproductive units, the movement away from a 'peasant' mode of production is one of the keys to our modern world. The English were never 'peasants' in the sense of combining the social and the economic units. And the educational system is the essential mechanism for turning the English away from peasanthood to the world of the autonomous individual.

The English invented several of the most important competitive team games – cricket, football, and rugby – and perfected others (horse racing, shooting, tennis). These games and sports combined 'contract' with 'status' in an unusual way; having entered the game contractually, the arena and rules create a competitive yet uniting sentiment. The games metaphor and mentality is found through much of English society in its law, politics, society and economic activity. The English also have the leisure and wealth to develop many hobbies.

A culture dominated by play – games, hobbies and passions – is strongly encouraged in English education. Clearly the English educational system, with its obsession with play of various kinds, was both a mirror and preparation for such a culture. Our school songs, and compulsory games almost every day, and the constant play in the playground was a training for life.

The unusually fragmented kinship system did not form the infrastructure of society. Children were sent away from home when they were young. They married for love. They placed the relationship with their married partner before that to their parents or children. In practice most people interacted with non-kin networks in religion, politics and economy. The English family system was unique in Europe and later spread to America and over much of the world. Friends replaced kin as the most important contacts, but patron-client relations were weak.

The cultural effects of the educational system spread everywhere and one effect was in the area of romantic love, another strong peculiarity of modernity, where many people choose their own marriage partners on the basis of physical and character attraction rather than having their marriages arranged by the wider family.

All of this, of course, fits exactly with the educational system. By separating people from their deep ties to parents, I and others, were left with an emotional and social gap. We had to learn how to find meaning through friendship, that is lasting bonds with strangers, and hence finding a substitute for what is usually done by the family.

A central feature of modernity is the development of associations based on 'contract,' rather than communities based on birth and blood. There has been an enormous growth of clubs, associations and other groupings. The development of legal Trusts and 'trust' from medieval times in England gave such activities the foundation on which they could develop, forming the underpinning of Anglo-American society. One particular example is the meeting place – the inn, the pub, the tea and coffee shops.

All this was taught to us at school. We were consciously taught how to be effective members of non-family associations at our schools. This was linked to the wider development of legal trusts, forming enduring co-working groups based on 'trust' of strangers, which lied behind a huge amount of modern British life, from religious to social, political and economic institutions. We were taught to be associational animals, undergoing this training in the very institutions (private schools and universities for example) which had been founded on the Trust principle. The charitable trusts, successors to the monastic organization based on another, religious, principle, taught us to shape our lives within the mutual fellowships of various kinds based on trust.

Turning to the question of political rights and the origins of democracy, often equated with 'modernity,' it is obvious to historians and others that almost always power becomes more centralized and absolutist, as in the history of all of continental Europe, China and many other civilizations.

It is equally obvious that England had a unique form of 'centralized feudalism' which was both directed to the centre but distributed much power to the lower levels. Without a permanent army, with the King under the Law, with a small paid bureaucracy it developed the first real 'democracy' along unusual lines. Later it governed its huge Empire in a similar way.

This is reflected in the schooling I and many others received. I was brought up in a system which I found in my first schools and later throughout my life working in universities. I would have found if I had later moved into the civil service and national government, industrial or financial services, the law or the church. It was the basis of the system used to hold together the huge British Empire, namely the system of delegated government, using the local leaders to rule and hence obviating the need for a heavy political bureaucracy from the centre.

From my experience, schools and universities were based on a great deal of delegated power and open discussion of troubling issues. They tended to be light on bureaucracy and heavy on promoting an ethic of oral and customary law which governed us in the absence of formal, written, rules. They were founded on an ideal of fairness and judging each case on its merits. Corruption in its various forms – nepotism, favoritism, bribery, coercion, patron-clientalism, were all remarkably absent from my experience from kindergarten to university. The fact that England was the mother of modern democracy and has, when compared to almost all other political systems been singularly free of rampant and seriously destructive corruption, is clearly a product of the educational system.

The legal system of England is one of the most significant features of its modernity. The unique mixture of Common Law and Equity, with judge-made, precedent-based, law, with the presence of juries and the assumption of innocence until proven guilty and the absence of torture, is fundamental. There was equality before the law and the rule of law. It was a legal system with particular sophistication in its treatment of personal rights and duties and the holding of property. This was the system, which underpinned modern rational capitalist economy and politics. Over the centuries it became totally different from that anywhere else in Europe.

Although we did not learn much explicitly about all this at school and university, unless we studied the history of England where legal changes loomed large, we learnt how to operate within the assumptions and mechanisms of the system indirectly. We learnt about fairness and equity, innocence until proved guilty, the fact that those in power, even up to the headmaster, were under the law. We all had our rights, even as little boys. We were quick to point out to teachers that something was not fair.

We should not be tortured. Our bodies and our spirits were our private property, as were our basic possessions. Disputes should be settled by argument and discussion, not by brute force. Everyone was under the law. The legal universe of English common law and equity fits perfectly with what I learnt in and out of the classroom from my first school through to nearly half a century of teaching at Cambridge.

People cannot be united either in a nation or in a great

Empire by formal contractual ties; they need a feeling of loyalty. The unusual English educational system, especially the unique custom of sending children off very young to be educated by others, provided this. It is both old and central in generating the sentiments of a modern society composed of individuals and strangers, who yet feel some common identity, not based on locality or blood.

It also constructed the character and system of authority for later life. It was later adapted as the device for holding together the 'imagined' empire across the globe when young children were sent home to be shaped into British identity through ten years of boarding education.

At school the English learnt a particular language which both reflected and shaped their view of the world. It is flexible, practical, egalitarian, non-gendered and capable of producing great poetry and prose. The use of irony and satire was much developed and a curious playful sense of humour was widespread. It is a language which has been carried all over the world.

Looking back on my education, both in and out of the classroom, I am surprised at how much stress was placed on this socio-linguistic training. A love of literature, a heavy emphasis on all forms of humour, from satire to wit, a scorn of the ridiculous, a playing with words, a delight in the beauty of nature, a fascinations with people's characters, explored in our analysis of novels, these and many other things were shaped by my education. And, of course, the skills of speaking, both the grammatical structures as well as the accents, which placed us in an appropriate social bracket for further progress in the future were central.

The schools were machines for turning us into people who

could both appreciate the world around us and express our thoughts in a way which would convince others of our gentlemanly standing. They were preparing us for rhetorical power which would be essential in any professional walk of life.

All this I learnt along with my British identity, something I shared across geographical regions and across class and which was one of the main reasons I had been sent home from India. I became 'English' in my accent, jokes, sense of the past, morality and mentality. Anywhere I went later in life would become just a temporary residence 'abroad.' 'Home' was always Britain and I was deeply moved by my country's native literature and proud, even when recognizing lapses, of it history when I compared it to the history of others. I tried to avoid becoming a 'Little Englander,' for I felt a citizen of the wide Empire too. But at my core I was British – British because my Scottish roots were nearly as strong as my English.

The unusual wealth and especially the rapid growth in the eighteenth century in both agricultural and industrial output depended considerably on the application of 'reliable knowledge,' or 'science,' to practical matters such as wind and water power generation, steam engines and other machines, the rationalization of agriculture through fertilizers and breeding of superior animals. So the growth of knowledge and techniques, and especially the institutions of knowledge including universities was important, and was part of that triangle of 'knowledge: technology: mass production: knowledge,' which lies behind modern growth.

The growth of understanding of the world through science and technology has been a notable feature of English development from medieval scientists like Roger Bacon, through Newton and Darwin, to many outstanding Nobel prize winners today. The system of education, both in schools and universities, which encouraged questioning, testing of evidence, logic and open enquiry without people being crushed by tradition, religion, or political pressures, is clearly central to what has happened. Whereas the promise of the Renaissance faded over much of Europe and the great medieval universities were turned into state institutions, in England the educational system was both an expression and a cause of the flourishing of an unusual 'open' intellectual world.

Certainly I know from my own experience that I was always encouraged, even challenged and pushed, to be imaginative, innovative and to challenge conventional wisdom. I never feared that my ideas would be used against me as a person. It is easy to take this for granted until we consider the majority of human societies where education, rather than being liberating and encouraging of open thought, is a machine to indoctrinate and suppress all questioning of the deeper assumptions of a religious or political system.

Formal religion has declined on the surface of much of Britain today, but all of British society is deeply soaked in the metaphysical underpinnings of Christianity. This was a common European heritage, incorporating much from Greek and Roman philosophy. But in England a religion which was in a confrontation with the State from its start, and which emphasized the ethical dimensions of life, was particularly pronounced. Here many of the multitude of sects, Quakers, Methodists and many others, developed their own interpretations and thrived. Christianity was an essential foundation for the development of scientific thought. It also, as Weber argued, provided a necessary, if not sufficient, ingredient in the development of capitalism.

Although on the surface there has been much disunity and argument, scepticism and even atheism in England over the centuries, at its core a version of Christianity has been a central underpinning of much that is English. Yet religion as an organization was not dominant. At the Dragon school there was not even a Chapel, though we were taught the bible and said prayers every day. Religion within bounds, as a part of life, in moderation, yet valuable in parts for its ethics and the beauty of some of its features, was what we learnt.

Yet religion was the background to the schooling, in a similar way to the weather. Neither were oppressive or determining. We had a sense that there were Powers which we did not understand, there was some inner watcher, a God who would be pleased or displeased by our actions when no one else was watching. We were held up to higher standards in our schooling, but not threatened with damnation, the Inquisition or the infallibility of priests or the Pope.

I experienced a tolerant mixture of Anglican, Quaker, Methodist, earnest and quit gentle. So the education was more about the education of a Christian gentleman than just a Christian minister. Our family had nothing to do with it, for we broke with them. So there were no ancestors to worship, few family rituals (apart from baptism, marriage and funerals). We were on our own in religion to chose what to achieve and follow. Our education introduced us to a Christian option. Yet through my life I was taught to question and challenge the dogma I was being presented with.

The combined effects of all that has been described before

led to a strangely contradictory national character – or even, as David Hume suggested, the absence of any uniform national character at all. The English were simultaneous individualistic and conformist, shy and extrovert, lazy and restless, childish and mature, insecure and self-confident, gentle and brutal. These are the contradictions of modernity.

The effects of the educational system on English character is very strong. The English were full of contradictory personality, both aggressive and peaceful, repressed and extrovert, childish and mature, lonely and playful with others, is largely explained by their education.

* * *

I shall examine two of the wider consequences of becoming modern in a little more detail. One is the effect of rationality, defined in Weber's sense of 'instrumental' rationality, that is an effective relation between means and ends. If one wants to effect something, thought and action are increasingly 'rational' as they contribute to that end. To kill someone, one can use effective or ineffective means; to make money or grow crops, likewise the means can be rational or irrational. The question of whether the end or goal is 'rational' is another question.

The basic point is that the separation of spheres into economic, ideological, political and social allows 'rationality' (in terms of the relation of means to ends) to be greater. If one wants to make money, or to think new thoughts, or to choose a wife, it is often more 'rational' to do this without feeling the pressure which the mixing of spheres necessarily creates. For example, an astute trader can enter into contracts with others without constantly having to check or share his gains with his family and consulting them on all his moves; a person can plant the crops he thinks best at the time that is most suitable without worrying about religious or social pressures; a person can vote for whichever party she thinks will best represent her without pressure from priests or parents.

In effect, the rationality of most of the key institutions of modernity – parliamentary democracy ('free' voting), 'free' labour, transacting in a 'free' market economy, the 'freedom' of religious beliefs and speech, the 'freedom' to pursue truth, individual conscience and high social mobility – all of these are based on this kind of 'rationality.' It allows an individual to pursue a goal of a specific kind in a neutral way; priests, parents or bosses do not tell you how to vote or marry or do business. That is your choice.

It is this, many believe, which is one of the main sources of flexibility and hence dynamism in modern societies. Constant efforts are made to increase the autonomy of spheres, to fight off or reduce corruption, which is a word which basically means the unacceptable mixing or re-mixing of areas – allowing family pressures and links to enter politics or economics for example.

Yet there are also costs, as Max Weber also recognized in his concepts of 'disenchantment' and the iron cage of bureaucracy. One cost is that life can become rather meaningless or pointless. People can become very efficient at making large sums of money, but if that is the only goal, does it bring happiness? Or they may become politically powerful, but eaten up with power and with little other purpose.

One of the advantages of a world where spheres are blended is that every action or thought has overtones, acts like a part of a harmony in music, rather than a single note. A gift has 'spirit,' a kiss or a smile, a small gesture always signifies other things. Life feels enriched when everything we do seems to have social, symbolic and other meanings and is not just stripped to a bare, instrumental, functional means-ends relation. So the greyness, anxiety and loss of purpose which has often been detected in modern life is related to hyper-rationality.

Fortunately, however, humans have developed many actions which are absorbing and fulfilling, often collaborative and ends in themselves and not means to another end; games, arts, music, reading, hobbies, appreciation of nature and love are among these. So these control the defects of loneliness, unite the lonely crowd in often 'useless' but rewarding activities.

* * *

This takes me to the second effect of growing separation and individuation, namely the necessity of replacing status or birth-given bonds with contractual and individually made ones. How this was to be done was one of the central concerns of much of the social thinking from the nineteenth century onwards as it became clear from the growth of capitalism and urbanism and the destruction of the 'Ancien Regime' that a new order was emerging.

For most of the past, the people with whom one interacted to perform most actions, whether practical or symbolic, farming, worshipping or playing, were given at birth. One inter-acted with family and co-residents in a community.

Yet once this has been broken, the great move from status to contract has occurred, how do we set up 'action-sets,' 'networks' of strangers, fellowships and associations? What can help autonomous individuals form into entities which re-incorporate them, that is make into one body (corpus) again, while preserving the hard-achieved autonomy and freedom of the individual? Here it seems is one of the keys to successful modernity. The English developed a range of alternatives to fixed status groups. Many of their solutions combined co-operation with individual freedom. The ways in which this was done are quite different from the principle methods used in still basically non-modern civilizations.

In many half-modern cases, for example throughout much of the Mediterranean region as noted by anthropologists, patron-client or fictive kinship (making non-kin into 'honorary' kin, as with godparents) developed. This made many kinds of alliance possible, but the ties tended to be between just two individuals (dyadic). They created networks, 'friends' or 'patrons' and even 'friends of friends'. But they did not create effective groupings of people who worked for a common cause over a long period.

The English solutions lay in a series of devices to which we give terms such as fellowship, association, trust and club. All these have played an important part in my life and it is now obvious to me that much of my learning at school and university was about how to join and operate in such artificially, yet emotionally meaningful, semi-groups, which are collectively termed 'civil society', that is the wide range of bodies which lie between the individual and the State – churches, clubs, colleges and companies.

It is this 'civil society' which can initially threaten the State and hence it is attacked and destroyed by all absolutist systems, whether of the right or left. Yet, when it is successfully instituted in a balanced way, 'civil society' makes it possible for the miracle to occur whereby a few people acting closely and trustingly together and sharing their skills, ideas and efforts can achieve much more as a 'team' than they can individually. The sum of the parts is much greater than the parts themselves.

Such a 'corporation' (corpus is latin for body) is based on a delicate matter of trust, acceptance of some limitations of excessive individualism, the rejection of 'free-riding.' It leads to satisfaction because life becomes multi-stranded and purposeful through the 'social love' side of human nature, the desire to be approved and appreciated by other human beings, so that the rewards are not merely practical – a wonderful concert, a boat race football match or battle won, a great scientific discovery, a successful economic company – but the sharing of this with others.

The smallest example or microcosm of this phenomenon is the partnership of husband and wife in companionate marriage, where each forgoes some of his/her self to achieved a unified and greater good. Such a marriage is an equal, but joint relationship, where each contributes different things. That dyadic partnership is then amplified in all the associations of civil society.

What is different from the patron-client ties of many half-modern civilizations is that these civil society groupings are not just networks or one-to-one dyads. A patron-client relationship is just that – two people, even though each may have other patrons and other clients. It is a single, and often more or less single-stranded, reciprocity-based 'contract.' Likewise a flat version of this is the 'friends of friends' or guanxi of China, where one sets up a specific, contractual, relationship with another, or with a network. This may just be A and B, or possible one may then link up with C, D and E, who are friends of B.

In the end, these types of relationship, whether unequal (patron-client) or 'equal' (guanxi, mates, friends of friends) are based on measured and direct exchanges of favours between separated and discrete individuals. They are not very different from exchanges in the market. There need, for example, be no warmth or sense of long-term belonging, no sharing in the success of the other.

What is unusual about the type of organization which I am trying to describe is that the individual is merged, to a certain degree, in the greater whole, yet also retains his or her distinctive character and is not to be oppressed or coerced against his will by the collective. Obvious examples are rowing crews, football teams, drama societies, orchestras, firms and companies, colleges, church congregations and clubs of all kinds. In each of these cases some kind of named entity is set up with a continuing existence through time and an open and visible presence – the Bach Choir, Manchester United Football Club, King's College Cambridge, Lloyds Bank, the Athenaeum Club, St John's Church.

People through various voluntary agreements are either asked to join or join through their own choice. Once members, they find that they are expected to do and not to do certain things. There are rules of membership and the possibility of expulsion. There is usually some jointly owned property – a Church, College, Club House, Factory, which is jointly run by officers elected by the members.

Membership of such a unit both inhibits excessive individualism and creates responsibilities of membership, it absorbs a certain amount of energy and initiative and private enthusiasm. Yet by pooling effort, a boat can be rowed, a concert performed, students taught, money made, in a way which a lone individual could not possibly achieve.

It might be thought that this associational art would come easily, but in fact it has to be learnt. Children learn, in almost all civilizations, how to operate within a birth-given set of kin or caste structures, how to address and behave towards a mother's brother in a different way to the behaviour to a father's brother; how to treat upper and lower castes, nobles and peasants. In a modern society, an individual must learn through their 'education' how to operate within a much more flexible, ever-changing, set of relations with people who start as strangers, but on whom one is very quickly dependent.

For example, when you join an orchestra, relations with all the other players and the conductor must be learnt. When I joined a Cambridge college I had to learn the rules and relationships within the Fellowship, and how to deal with the officers of the college and the staff. There are always a dizzying number of permutations and possibilities in these complex situations and the rules and customs are often unspoken. The art one has to learn early in life is the generic skill of adapting to working closely with strangers, of turning such hitherto unknown people into trusted colleagues, if not close friends.

I now realize that this is precisely this art which was in many ways at the heart of my, and most people's, English education. The boarding schools are an extreme form of this education, placing the pupil in a total environment of communal living with strangers. The shock, speed and density of going as a little boy into a dormitory, common room, playing ground, playing field and school room and learning how to survive is a preparation for the many shifting memberships of various 'clubs' or artificial groups of some kind one will later operate in.

Yet in a wider way it is not just in boarding schools that this happens, though the elite training in 'clubability' is most extreme there. This training happens in all schools, from kindergarten onwards, as I see from my own children and grandchildren who have been through state day schools. The child is trained in membership of numerous sub-sets and groups, learning to work in teams as well as individually.

To get to the mass proliferation of civil society, which is the necessary underpinning, the under-carpet of a modern civilization, and making individualistic modernity tolerable is not at all easy. There are many obstructing institutions, many forces which wish to preserve their monopolies, whether of a status kind (caste, kinship), a religious kind (fundamentalisms of all kinds) or powerful, centralized, political systems (absolute states, right and left).

All of these would like to block and destroy both the final proliferation of trust-based and collaborate units which strengthen ordinary individuals in their pursuit of non-State goals. Consequently they are particularly suspicious of educational systems which are recognized to be the generators of civil society. Hence the banning of female education in many fundamentalist societies.

Competing institutions know that Francis Bacon was right - 'knowledge is power.' And they think that since power is a finite force, there is a zero sum game whereby all civil institutional entities drain away power. If entities are allowed to exist independently of the family, religion or State, where will it end ?

Hence it is often only indirectly, a football club in Afghanistan, a youth orchestra combining Palestinians and Israelis – that the jealous eyes of those who want to monopolize an individual's allegiance can be averted.

Yet modernity cannot thrive if all it consists of is molecular individuals. The special purpose of 'clubs' and 'Trusts' and associations (games, music, learning, religion) which have a voluntary 'congregation' or membership, make modernity both bearable and effective. Trust breeds trust, friendship engenders sociality and hence meaning, and all this increases creativity and efficiency in a modern society is about shaping both the individual (self love) and the social being (social love).

* * *

Putting this in another way, in a pre-modern society, where education is largely about moving a person from one status to another, even when it is, as in traditional China, sometimes from peasant to mandarin, or in France from son of a lawyer to a lawyer and head of a lawyer's household, there is no need or desire to use the early years as a time to train people for 'Society,' using 'Society' to mean civilizations based mainly on the inter-action between strangers. There is no need to train people for civil society for it hardly exists. All organizations, in so far as they exist, are determined by birth in some way – one Church, an occupation based on the family, a political view based on family alliances. The setting up of new associations on the model of a club is not what happens.

Yet when I went to the Dragon and then Sedbergh and Oxford,

I soon learnt that most of the success in my life depended on my ability to develop social skills – it is not what you know, but who you know. Success in the dormitory, day room, play ground, playing field, stage or classroom even, depended largely on team work – learning to follow, share and lead.

So the proliferation of numerous groups to which I belonged, formal and informal, self-created or pre-existing, which absorbed most of my waking hours from school onwards, and which were not related to my family, was what was important. These groups played a great deal, play and games being the archetypical activity of associations, from marbles in the playground to the House of Commons or King's College, Cambridge, from the playing fields of Eton to the Battle of Waterloo.

Our group 'play' demanded commitment, trust, shared effort and gave us shared rewards in praise and delight. At their best they stimulated creativity within the rules, evolutionary selections of accidental improvements, combined talents which no single human being can possess.

* * *

So it might be argued that modernity as a separation of spheres is based on contradictions. On the side of rationality, it demands strong means/ends rationality, severely practical, common-sense and goal directed. Power requires political means, wealth requires economic, belief requires religion. Yet the contradiction is that to restore richness and meaning to our lives, alongside these, there are many intensely pursued but 'useless', in some ways 'irrational' passions – games, art, music, hobbies, walking, writing and many others.

There is also a contradiction in terms of associations. While the individual is the only place where the interaction of spheres occurs, and hence there is 'molecular individualism' and almost unlimited 'freedom' in theory. Yet combined with this self-love, there must be a rich proliferation of organizations based on social love, that is the surrendering of some of our freedom in exchange for others doing the same thing. This pooling – 'casting bread upon the waters' in the belief that the bread will return in an augmented form, long-term (general) reciprocities and generosity, mixed with feelings of honour, responsibility, sacrifice of short-term gains, the code of the gentleman - is something which makes the individual billiard balls into an effective assembly.

These contradictions can be studied through how we are socialized. At school and home I was being given opposite messages and had to learn to integrate them in my mind and character. Be true to yourself, retain your individual judgement, stick to your principles, strive to be free. But also think of others, surrender to others for a greater good, find your greatest reward in the happiness of others.

Be careful, rational, calculating and methodical. Break problems into parts, proceed along logical chains, separate out thought and context, all these are rational strategies. But at the same time I was encouraged to retain a sense of mystery, of beauty, of love, of childlike innocence, spend time on many things which are of no utilitarian value, even wasteful and 'irrational'. Again much of my education was trying to fill me with this double message, the implications of which I had to resolve in my own way.

SEVEN

English and Continental Education

I HAVE ARGUED that the essence of modernity is the separation of religion from politics, and of economy from society. This was both reflected in and manufactured by the system of socialization of children, including formal education. The most extreme example of this English system, found at its height in the century between the middle of the nineteenth and twentieth centuries, was in the British boarding public schools. Let us see what four foreign observers made of them: two are French, one Belgian and one Austrian. They wrote books about England published between 1872 and 1946.

One of the most important observations on the relations between schools and family is made by the Belgian author Émile Cammaerts (1878-1953) who later became Professor of Belgian Studies in the University of London in 1933. In his *Observations on England*, published in 1930, he laid stress on the central difference between continental and English education. This is that in continental education there is a strict division between the home, which is the place for wider education (social, moral) and the school for just intellectual education. In England, especially in the boarding schools, it was very different.

Cammaerts wrote that 'Moral education, which has hitherto been the basis of English training, is left to home influence abroad and takes no active part in school life. The same applies to a great extent, to sport.'[1] Cammaerts expands this as follows: 'Apart from religious schools, which only influence a minority, secondary and higher education abroad is confined to the intellectual training of the student. After obtaining his degree, the latter will become an efficient lawyer, doctor or engineer, but he will only be a gentleman if he has been lucky enough to be born into a refined family.'[2]

In continental education the school is not about training character, deportment, manners, accent and all the things that denote one's social class. It is about technical tools for a job. In England, he suggests, it is a broad spectrum, trying to fashion a particular type of person.

This account links the crucial separation of home and school in most educational systems, compared to the total role of the school in England, to the social class differences. For Cammaerts continues that the continental system 'would have proved disastrous in a country in which the aristocracy has remained the most influential power in the State, and in which ranks of this upper class have to be reinforced with new recruits every year.' In England education makes you a gentleman, forms the character of the elite group. In continental countries it does not change your social status, which is entirely determined by your family. Education itself is of a technical kind; it is about acquiring the skills suitable to your position. Lawyers will educate their children to be lawyers, teachers children will be teachers and so on. It is about acquiring skills and not character.

---

[1] ÉMILE CAMMAERTS, *Discoveries in England*, 1930, p. 119.
[2] Ibid., p. 133.

A second observer is the French critic and historian Hippolyte Taine (1828-1893), whose *Notes on England* were published in 1872. Taine notes that English public-schools (he particularly wrote about Harrow which he visited) provide a home rather than temporary barracks. 'Thus a boy, when he first arrives at school, finds himself in something like his own paternal household, the more so in that English families are numerous. He has a home of his own, dines within three paces of a lady (housemaster's wife or daughter) is, in short, a person among people. He lives in a natural, whole environment and is not, as with us, subject to a barrack-like communism.'[3]

The difference in function between a general-purpose 'home from home' of an English boarding school and the 'think-tank' in France can be found in the architecture and surroundings of the schools, as Taine explains.:

'...in France a lycée is a large, stone box into which you enter by means of a single hole provided with an iron gate and a porter. Inside are a few courtyards like playgrounds, occasionally a wretched stand of trees but, on the other hand, a great many walls. Since the said box is always in a large town, the young man who once passes its iron gate is confronted inside and out, by nothing but bricks and mortar. Whereas here [Harrow] the school is a small town by itself, with numerous ways open to the country. At Eton I noticed that the walls about the big central courtyard were covered with roses, creepers and honeysuckle: beyond lie lush meadows where monster elms spread their age-old branches....'

---

3   HIPPOLYTE TAINE, *Notes on England,* 1957, p. 101.

This basic contrast of school placing and openness does not only apply to the public school stage. Most preparatory schools are built in the countryside. The same contrast also extends at the other way, with many universities, particularly Oxford and Cambridge, built in rural towns.

Taine then describes the sporting and outdoor life of the boys at Harrow. 'Now it is a most important advantage for the body, imagination, mind and character to be able to develop in a wholesome and tranquil atmosphere in conformity with the blind requirements of their instincts.' [1]

Taine then talks about the freedom of the boys, in control of their own time, describing how the boarding school prepares boys for the future in what we would now perhaps describe as an individualistic, capitalistic, competitive, yet orderly and co-operative society.

> *'On the whole, then, human nature is treated here with more respect and is less interfered with. Under the influence of an English education boys are like the trees in an English garden; under that of our own, like the pleached and pollarded trees of Versailles. Here, for instance, schoolboys are almost as free as undergraduate. They are required to be present in class, for study, and for dinner, and to be in by a certain time at night but no more. The rest of the day is their own, and it is up to them to employ this leisure as they please. The only task which must be done in their free time is a certain amount of "home-work" but this they can do where and when they like. They may work in their own rooms or elsewhere…They are masters of their time and also of their money, treat themselves to*

---

[1] TAINE, *Notes on England*, p. 102.

snacks and buy things to decorate their rooms. It seems that if they run into debt, their small matter of privately owned furniture or furnishings is sold by auction. Initiative and responsibility: it is curious to see babies of twelve raised to the dignities of manhood.'[2]

More than the physical freedom, it is the political and social structure of the school which educates the child. Taine examines team games and sports and concludes,

'Here then, thus early, are the seeds of the spirit of association, an apprenticeship in both obedience and command, since every cricket team accepts a discipline and appoints a leader. But this principle is applied very much more widely; boys and youths together form an organised body, a sort of small, distinct State with it own chiefs and its own laws. The chiefs are the pupils in the highest class ('sixth form'), more especially the fifteen highest pupils in the school ('monitor') and, in each house, the highest pupil. They maintain order, see that the rules are obeyed and, in general, do the same work as our ushers. They prevent the strong from bullying the weak, are arbitrators in all disputes, take a hand when a small boy gets into some kind of trouble with a villager or a shop-keeper, and punish delinquents. In short, pupils in England are governed by pupils; and each one, having first been subject to authority, comes in due course to wield it. During his final year each is enrolled on the side of the rules, the law, and it becomes his business to see that it is respected; he learns its value,

---

2 TAINE, *Notes on England*, pp. 102-3.

and adopts it of his own free will, instead of kicking against it, which is what a French schoolboy would not fail to do.'[1]

The result is that the boy is becoming a man, character-wise, and not just being intellectually trained: this is the huge difference with continental education as he saw it. Taine writes that

'... *in England there is no wide separation between the boy and the grown man; school, and the great world, are on the same footing with no wall or ditch between them, so that the one prepares for and leads to the other. The adolescent does not, as in France he does, emerge from a forcing-house, from a special atmosphere... He has not only been cultivating his mind, he has been undergoing an apprenticeship for adult life. In politics and in religion he finds, at twenty years of age, forms and structures for which his tastes and faculties have been adapted in advance.*'[2]

The effect, he believed, was to train people to understand how to fit into a democratic society. Taine noticed the result of this system. 'Consequently when they leave school and began their adult lives they are less inclined to consider the rules absurd and authority ridiculous. They reconcile liberty and subordination, are nearer to an understanding of the conditions in which a society can exist and the rights and duties of a citizen.'[3]

It is achieved at some expense, however, especially in the nineteenth and early twentieth centuries, for schools could be Darwinian selecting grounds, red in tooth and claw.

---

1 TAINE, *Notes on England*, p. 104.
2 Ibid., p. 105.
3 Ibid., p. 104.

A MODERN EDUCATION

'For, by and large, a school conducted on such lines is a sort of primitive society in which force reigns almost unchecked, the more so in that the oppressed makes it a point of honour never to denounce their oppressors. The masters intervene as little as possible: they are not, as they are in France, the standing representatives of humanity and justice. Very rarely, and only in some schools, may they be appealed to or the advice and aid of the oldest boys sought. The weak must fend for themselves, and must suffer in silence.'[4]

Part of this toughening up is the sparse physical conditions and the emphasis on sport. 'On the whole, education, on these terms, is not unlike that of the Spartans: it hardens the body and it tempers the character. But, as far as I can make out, it often produces (merely) sportsmen and louts…. It is not surprising that we should find many people attributing the wretched intellectual results we obtain to this mania for muscularity.'

Taine supports his picture of the primary emphasis on character formation rather than academic ability in England through a brief analysis of *Tom Brown's Schooldays*.

'Neither Tom nor his father were much concerned with education properly so-called. The father, wondering what last words of advice to give his son, reflects: "Shall I tell him to mind his work and say he's sent to school to make himself a good scholar? Well, but he isn't sent to school for that – at any rate not for that mainly. I don't care a straw for Greek particles, or the digamma: no more does his mother. What is he sent to school for? Well, partly because he wanted so to go.

---

4 TAINE, *Notes on England,* p. 110-11.

*If he'll only turn out a brave, helpful, truth-telling English-
man, and a gentleman, and a Christian, that's all I want.'*[1]

This is echoed by Tom Brown himself. 'And when Tom, after several years, asks himself what he went to school for, he comes, upon reflection, to this conclusion:

*'I want to be A1 at cricket and football and all the other
games, and to make my hands keep my head against any other
fellow, lout or gentleman – I want to carry away just as much
Latin and Greek as will take me through Oxford respect-
ably. – I want to leave behind me the name of a fellow who
never bullied a little boy, or turned his back on a big one.'*[2]

Taine's comment on Tom Brown's aims is apt.

*'Remarkable words, and they do sum up very well the ordinary
feelings of an English father and son: learning and the cultiva-
tion of the mind come last; character, heart, courage, strength
and physical address are in the first rank. Such an education turns out men capable of great moral and physical striv-
ings, with all the advantages, but likewise all the disadvan-
tages, of that particular orientation of body and soul.'*[3]

The result of the great difference between the goals of training the mind, or training the whole character, is described by Taine as follows:

---

1   TAINE, *Notes on England*, p. 106.
2   THOMAS HUGHES, *Tom Brown's Schooldays*, cited in TAINE, *Notes on England*, p. 106.
3   TAINE, *Notes on England*, p. 107.

'they [English] are both more childish and more manly than our boys: more childish in that they are fonder of games and less disposed to overstep the limits of their age; more manly in that they are more capable of decision and self-government. Whereas the French schoolboy, especially the boarder in our college is bored, soured, fined-down, precocious, far too precious. He is in a cage and his imagination ferments.'[4]

This is a great traditional difference in educational systems. The English is an apprenticeship for adulthood, in Taine's words, a total package, where one moves away from familistic integration. It becomes more important than the home in almost every way. It is clear from my own experience even at kindergarten, and certainly from the age of eight my most intense life was at school. Home increasingly became the place to rest and recover, a sort of 'holiday' from real life. That is why it was called the 'holidays' or later the 'vacation' at University.

What starts as just a marked predominance of the school in the preparatory period becomes more and more evident. By the age of 16 my public school overshadowed my home not only in my mental but also emotional and social life. When I left my public school I almost immediately left home, to go abroad first and later to get a job. I had effectively 'left' home, psychologically, even if I still had a base there. And this was even more marked a feature of Oxford, where the 'vacations' were far less important than the term times. My friends were at Oxford, rather than at my home and my emotional life was centred round it.

---

4   TAINE, *Notes on England,* p. 105.

* * *

Another way to pursue the same huge difference is to look at the contrast between education which is directed at the mind/brain – that is memory, logic, facts formal schooling – and education which is aimed at creating a certain kind of person.

This is pithily put by several authors. Lord Elgin said that education in England 'fits one for nothing and trains him for everything,' and C. G. Sampson wrote that 'the purpose of education is not to prepare children for their occupations but to prepare them against their occupations.'[1]

In Taine's word, it is an apprenticeship rather than a mere transmission of the content of one brain, one lump of facts and opinions, to another. The economist Marshall wrote 'The mere accumulation of knowledge stunts rather than educates the mind... (England) still holds a leadership, almost unchallenged except by other English speaking countries, in that education of character which is obtained from individual activities, rather than from instruction whether verbal or in print. The playground had a notable share in the 'real' education of her youth: and the paths of the ocean have been the Universities of an exceptional number of her men.'[2]

One simple index of the difference is the number of hours spent on academic work. Taine noted this in relation to England and France.

'A maximum of eight hours work a day; it is more likely to

---

1 C. G. SAMPSON, quoted in, HAROLD INNIS, *The Bias of Communication,* 1951, p. 204.
2 MARSHALL, 1923, quoted in, MOKYR, ed, *Industrial 300,* p. 96.

be six or seven. With us it is eleven, which is unreasonable. An adolescent needs physical exercise: it is against nature to force him to be all brain, a sedentary book-worm. Here, athletic games, fives, football, running, rowing and above all cricket take up a part of every day. Moreover classes end at noon two or three days a week to make time for games.'[3]

What is behind this is the goal of creating a certain character, the Christian, universalist, broadly competent, amateur, gentleman. The goal is never stated, as the Austrian traveller and writer Paul Cohen-Portheim (1880-1932) observes in his book *England the Unknown Isle*. Although Portheim is specifically talking about Oxford and Cambridge, what he writes is equally true of my public and preparatory schools.

'They are not so much places of instruction as training-grounds, their object being to mould the students' characters and form young men who shall continue the traditions of the ruling class as they have been formed in the course of centuries, in correspondence with the ideals of the English race. This aim has never been consciously formulated and is not set forth in any curriculum, simply because it is an assumption that is taken for granted.'[4]

The kind of medieval ideal is well described by Cammaerts. As he explains, not only is it very old, but it is applied to children as soon as they go to school, from about the age of seven or eight.

---

3   TAINE, *Notes on England*, p. 103.
4   PAUL COHEN-PORTHEIM, *England the Unknown Isle*, 1931, p. 97.

> *'There is a remarkable similarity between the rules of the medieval order of chivalry and the code of honour which an English boy of seven is urged to follow, as much by his older schoolfellows as by his masters... But he will have to be truthful and to keep his word. He must be generous. He must never retreat before the enemy. He must love his country. He must respect the weak and defend the oppressed, and fulfil his duties, if not towards his feudal lord at least towards his school. Football and cricket have taken the place of skirmishes and tournaments, but the two codes are essentially the same. This is the foundation on which the boy's character is built, and it lies so deep that, even if in later years faith deteriorates and sense of duty weakens, honour generally manages to survive....'*[1]

As Cammaerts observes, much of this code is learnt outside the classroom – lessons will not teach one to be brave, honourable, truthful and so on. A mathematical or linguistic skill teaches one nothing about morals. As in the poem 'play up and play the game,' the ethic is there in the deserts and in the mountains, in the heat of battle or in the calm times, whether in Bombay and the Himalayas, or in the Stock Exchange or Law Courts.

What is being inculcated is the product of the immensely powerful mechanisms which I have personally experienced in my own intense indoctrination in boarding institutions from eight to 21 and will describe in more detail later. The careful mixture of fear, praise, pain, pleasure, friendship, love and dislike produces a very deep 'habitus' or set of structuring forces in our lives. It creates the inner gyroscope of an

---

1 CAMMAERTS, *Discoveries*, p. 134.

'inner-directed' personality which Riesman analysed in 'The Lonely Crowd.'

By the time we reached University we were expected to have made these codes part of our nature. Some of its constituents are again described by Cammaerts. 'He must observe a material and moral etiquette. His soul must be as clean as his hands. His honour must be unstained. He must, above all, play fair and show his mettle. Insincerity is to be shunned, not so much because it is sinful as because it is mean and despicable. There is a tradition of generosity, open-handedness and courtesy to be observed.'[2] The theme is honesty, dependability, sincerity, a particular code of honour and etiquette which I recognize as being inculcated in me over the years.

One of the reasons for the self-patrolled nature of this training, its elements of freely given adherence to a self-imposed code, is that such a set of principles could not possibly be policed in adult life except by the individual. It is a code of a ruling elite who have no one except God above them. The whole point was that this kind of education was to train leaders of men (and women).

It was above all designed to be the training for the tiny proportion of the population who would become the professional classes. They would go to private schools or grammar school, to the top finishing academic like Oxford or Cambridge or Sandhurst or Adiscombe and learn the rules of leadership. This was precisely the role of 'public' (in other words 'private') schools – to train an upper class. And this was totally different from the continental model, according to Portheim. 'The function of

---

[2] CAMMAERTS, *Discoveries*, p. 123.

the Pubic Schools and the older universities is to educate the upper class that governs the country; they are opposed in their inner-most nature to the democratic character of the *gymnasium* or the modern university… and aim at the breeding of a select human type, selection being the antithesis of equal rights.'[1]

It is a system where, like other 'games,' you start with some sort of equality and turn this into temporary inequality. Humans are born with roughly equal talents and even, to a considerable extent, equal rights. Yet through breeding, some are chosen to rule, and the rest to obey. It is a long process, this learning the art of ruling, for the stresses will be heavy, especially for those who are involved in ruling the largest Empire the world has ever known.

Again Portheim notes the duration of the training. 'He has the greatest respect for the gentleman and very little for the specialist; but the gentleman is a specialist in the art of ruling, which is the aim and object of the education of the young Englishman of the upper class, the education that begins at the great Public Schools like Eton, Winchester and the rest and is completed at Oxford and Cambridge.'[2] In fact, it is not just something which starts with the public schools but, as I have found with study of my preparatory school, much of the work has already been done by the age of 13. Sedbergh, and then Oxford, were just a second and third re-beating and sharpening of the blade.

This emphasis on character building, and the fact that much of the 'education' came from activities outside the classroom,

---

[1] PORTHEIM, *England the Unknown Isle*, p. 107.
[2] Ibid,. p. 97.

is shown in a number of ways. The prime goal was to teach the inner-directed self-control, the freedom which comes from working within a framework of self-imposed and self-discovered customary codes and traditions. As Portheim wrote, 'liberty is only possible within a framework of laws, and English liberty consists in imposing these laws on oneself. They are the conventions, obedience to which the Englishman demands of himself and his neighbour, and they are just as binding as the rules of a game, no game being without rules....'[3] This is a part of the well-known self-control of the British gentleman. Taine noted the 'complete self-mastery, constantly maintained sang-froid, perseverance in adversity, serious-mindedness, dignity of manners and bearing, the avoidance of all affectation or swaggering....'[4]

Another French observer was Pierre Maillaud; *The English Way*, (1945), made some revealing observations on this. He wrote of the high degree of trust and lack of formal rules in England.

> '*The result is ... you have the difference between a community regulated to the last dot and overburdened with written rules, and one which is self-regulated by sheer respect of the social contract and which saves its energies for more creative or enjoyable activities than the control of citizens by other citizens. This principle of self-regulation which demands not only a code but a tradition is a characteristically English contribution to progress. It is one which does not defeat its own purpose as does a comprehensive control of life which, by making the*

---

3 PORTHEIM, *England the Unknown Isle*, p. 44
4 TAINE, *Notes on England*, p. 145.

performance of duty compulsory, divests it of all moral or social value and thus destroys the very basis of human progress.'[1]

The way in which this worked, as we have seen, was to leave children and adolescents to run their own lives. As he put it 'The spectacle of children making their own plans, arranging their own games, establishing their own codes, enjoying the freedom of a house, is common in England and rare on the Continent, just as the warm and inspiring atmosphere of a French family is seldom to be found in England.'[2]

---

1 PIERRE MAILLAUD, *The English Way*, 1945, p. 257.
2 Ibid., p. 69.

EIGHT

English and Chinese Traditional Education

A CENTRAL GOAL of the traditional Chinese educational system (which lasted, in essence, until the 1930s, and parts of which still exists) which, in some ways, in form, if not in content, makes it rather similar to the main goal of English elite education, was to construct a certain kind of moral and social character. It was the aim of Confucius and those who came after him to shape the ethically 'good' subject – that is good in relation both to the family and the State.

The point has often been made, but needs to be stressed since it is easy to be dazzled, as I was, by the huge emphasis on intellectual learning, and then to think that education and examinations were, as in the European Continental model, almost exclusively about just improving the mind. In fact, while the head was very important, it was in no way divorced from the heart in the Chinese case, just as the school was in no ways separated from the family. Family and school, head and heart, were fused together.

As Hughes put it: 'From most points of view it was an extremely intellectualist education… But the underlying principle of the whole was the making of a man, the development of personality and the training of moral character. The educated man took his stand before society as an expert in moral principles. In all the relationships of life, whether precedented or unprecedented, he was the man to point out the right word, the right act, the right ritual.'[1] The same point is made by Latourette. 'Its purpose was the growth of men and not the impartation of information. Its aim was cultural, not utilitarian, the self-development of the individual who was supposed to set an example. So, in theory at least, it made government almost unnecessary.'[2]

Finally, to drive home this most crucial of points, for I had not grasped it myself until starting this survey, it is worth quoting Williams. 'The great end of education, therefore, among the ancient Chinese, was not so much to fill the head with knowledge, as to discipline the heart and purify the affections. One of their writers says, "Those who respect the virtuous and put away unlawful pleasures, serve their parents and prince to the utmost of their ability, and are faithful to their word; these, thought they should be considered unlearned, we must pronounce to the educated men."'[3]

The Chinese aimed at character formation, but it was a different kind of character from the British. And the methods they used were totally at odds with what I had experienced. Finally, the relationship between the school's function and the home was entirely different in the two cases.

In relation to the goals of education, we shall see the difference working out below. Very briefly, I was to become an individualist, independent of my home and the wider group, self-confident, ingenious, competitive, creative, tough in mind

---

[1] E.R. HUGHES, *The Invasion of China by the Western World*, 1937, p. 157.
[2] KENNETH LATOURETTE, *The Chinese*, 1946, p. 793.
[3] S. WELLS. WILLIAMS, *The Middle Kingdom*, 1, 1883, p. 523.

and body. In China, the character to be formed was to be one which accepted hierarchy, was conformist, harmonious, learnt respect, eschewed competition, was to be aesthetic and grave. In both cases there was a powerful inculcation towards ethical responsibility, but it was a different ethic.

In relation to the methods of instilling this character, in my case I learnt most of what I should become outside the classroom. It is true, as I look back at it, that I can now see that embedded in my learning, in the poems and plays, in the history and theology, there was a set of strong messages about the person I was supposed to become. For example, as I see from my Chaucer, Shakespeare and Hazlitt work at Sedbergh, models of good and bad were constantly being placed before me.

Despite this, I had come to believe that it was in the non-intellectual settings, in the playground, the games field, the dormitories and studies, the hobbies, interests and friendships, that I learnt my character. So I had mistakenly thought that Chinese schools, which, seemed on the surface to belike Taine's description of enclosed French school, were just about the head.

What I now discover is that the Chinese embed the character and moral teaching inside the formal learning and in the attitudes to the staff and school environment. The reverence for the sensei and the grave rituals of learning, combine with the overbearing (to us) moral character of all the learning – one long sermon as we should think it – and it is there that a child learns what sort of person he should be.

The point is well made by Williams. He quotes one of the key textbooks for young children, the 'Juvenile Instructor' to the following effect: 'Another injunction is, "Let children always be taught to speak the simple truth; to stand erect and in their proper places, and listen with respectful attention." The way to become a student, 'is, with gentleness and self-abasement, to receive implicitly every word the master utters. The pupil, when he sees virtuous people, must follow them, when he hears good maxims, conform to them. He must cherish no wicked designs, but always act uprightly; whether at home or abroad, he must have a fixed residence, and associate with the benevolent, carefully regulating his personal deportment, and controlling the feelings of his heart.'[1]

When we come to examine the content of that was taught in schools, we shall see that (to us) an amazingly high proportion of what was taught was about morality, or social ethics and the models of character a child should follow. The facts were less important than the attitudes in the stories.

Another reason why I failed to see that Chinese traditional education was about character, as much as about intellectual formation, was that it does not fit either of the models I had formed of western elite education. In the standard continental system (except in some extreme religious schools) the school deals with the head, the home with the heart/character. In the English elite system, the school is both head and heart to a large extent. China is different, for the school and the home are undivided and both deal with the heart, though the school take over the head as well. Just as the Chinese, through Confucius, brought the Sate and the family into a single hierarchical line of duty, so that the duty to the father and Emperor reinforce each other, so the Chinese unified the training by using the school as an extension of the home and the home as an extension of the school.

The overlap can be seen in the crucial point at which children are first sent off to school. In England there is the transitional period – the kindergarten – where the home is still primary, but one is learning some of the disciplines of school. But then there was the shock of boarding school at age eight and all was changed.

The shift in China was different. The school became an extension of the home, like going off to spend time with a rather severe uncle. The teacher was one's (temporary) father – teaching skills which one father and mother did not have, or did not have time to impart. 'Boys commence their studies at the age of seven with a teacher; for, even if the father be a literary man he seldom instructs his sons, and very few mothers are able to teach their offspring to read. Maternal training is supposed to consist in giving a right direction to the morals, and enforcing the obedience of the child....'[2]

So there was no break, no opposition, no split – unlike the western tradition.

The anthropologist Francis Hsu, makes the same point: 'American children, when they begin school, for the first time come into close contact with persons, ideas, and activities over which the parents exercise little or no control... The Chinese child, having never been set apart from the world of his elders, faces no such trial.... This means that the Chinese child not only finds satisfaction of all his social needs in the kinship group

---

2 WILLIAMS, *The Middle Kingdom*, 1, p. 521.

where he begins life, but he is also under no compulsion to leave it as he grows up.'[1]

This causes not only a clash between systems, but also a clash in the child's own identity and memory of the past and the present – something I felt strongly. 'The second difficulty facing the American child in school, at least among the middle and upper classes, is the gap between an idealized childhood world and the real world.'[2]

The western child has to learn to be independent of parents – to break the tie, reject the family with all its implications. The Chinese child always remained in the same relationship to his/her parents for life. Here, I suspect, India and China have a shared basic position.

* * *

Concentrating on the common schools (and some private schools) for the earlier years, what were they like? They feel very different from English schools in a number of respects. Classes, whether at school or in the social sense, are at the heart of English society – and make it easier to teach groups of students, or to deal with segments of the population. Thus I am amazed to find that there were no such things as classes in Chinese schools – though perhaps their small size in a single room helps to explain this.

The absence in China is described by Williams. 'When the lads come together at the opening of the school, their attainments

---

1 Francis Hsu, *Americans and Chinese*, 1955, p. 105 and 115.

2 Hsu, *Americans and Chinese*, p. 108.

are ascertained; the teacher endeavours to have his pupils nearly equal in this respect, but inasmuch as they are all putto precisely the same tasks, a difference is not material.'[3] The same absence is elaborated by Dyer Ball: 'there was no class system in Chinese schools; each boy formed a class by himself: there were as many classes as there were boys. A dull scholar was thus not drawn on faster than he was able to go by the quicker boys, nor did the brighter pupils have a drag on their progress in the persons of the dull ones.'[4]

Much of English schooling is about doing examinations in the schools, gaining prizes, being given some sort of qualification. Another difference is that all of that was absent in Chinese schools. There was, of course, a vast examination system run by the State. But it was entirely separate from the schools. Thus Williams explains that 'No public examinations take place in either day or private schools, nor do parents often visit them, but rewards for remarkable proficiency are occasionally conferred. There is little gradation of studies, nor are any diplomas conferred on students to show that they have gone through a certain course.'[5]

Another difference is the absence of teaching aids in Chinese schools. Although many of these aids may be relatively modern even in the West, it would probably be the case that in elite education in eighteenth or nineteenth century Europe there would be some use of visual aids. This was not the case in China: 'the furniture of the school merely consists of a desk and a stool for

---

3   WILLIAMS, *The Middle Kingdom*, 1, p. 526.
4   DYER BALL, *Things Chinese*, 1989, p. 207.
5   WILLIAMS, *The Middle Kingdom*, 1, p. 546.

each pupil, and an elevated seat for the master, for maps, globes, blackboards, diagrams, etc., are yet to come in among its articles of furniture. In one corner is placed a tablet or an inscription on the wall, dedicated to Confucius and the god of Letters; the sage is styled the "Teacher and Pattern for All Ages," and incense is constantly burned in honour of them both.'[1] The last comment about incense makes one realize that there was an element of a sacred space about the school – a feeling we have had in some of the ancestor halls we have visited which we were told were used as school rooms in the past.

The sacredness, or at least very strong sense of dealing with older, ancestral, figures to be reverenced, can also be seen in the relations with the teacher. These relations are still different from that in the West. My English teachers were older, perhaps wiser, but ultimately not to be deeply revered – we could argue with them, even become sort of friends with them and at the Dragon School called them by nicknames. In China and Japan the teacher was *sensei* or guru, and my students from Japan call me *sensei* all their lives.

The teachers were to be revered and treated with the utmost respect and awe. They were surrogates of the State and of the Family. They were fathers and Emperors in their little kingdoms. Much of the teaching was to inculcate this Confucian ideal of respect for those above one in the political and family chain. And so the manner of the teachers and the rituals of the school were relevant to learning the power of authority.

This was reflected in the qualities which a teacher should have. 'The requisite qualifications of a teacher are gravity,

---

[1] WILLIAMS, *The Middle Kingdom*, 1, p. 525.

severity, and patience, and acquaintance with the classics; he has only to teach the same series of books in the same fashion in which he learned them himself and keep a good watch over his charge.'[2] Their authority was preserved by the two great forces which keep people in awe – physical and ritual coercion.

* * *

Another significant difference seems to have been in the intensity of the classroom experience. The long hours of formal learning, the absence of play periods and games, the short holidays, the long homework, all these are causes of worry in Korean, Japanese and Chinese schools to this day – and the pressures may be worse than ever as the syllabus broadens and the competition for top universities becomes more intense. In comparison, the limited hours, the play, games and music and other activities, the longer holidays, the absence of crammers, all are features of English elite education. It appears that this is an ancient difference.

Williams outlines the school day as follows: 'the first hours of study are from sunrise till ten AM, when the boys go to breakfast; they reassemble in an hour or more, and continue at their books till about five PM, when they disperse for the day. In summer, they have no lessons after dinner, but an evening session is often held in the winter, and evening schools are occasionally opened for mechanics and others who are occupied during the day.'[3] This suggests winter hours of up to 12

---

[2] WILLIAMS, *The Middle Kingdom*, 1, p. 526.

[3] Ibid.

hours of desk study and ten hours in the summer. This is very long – the English school hours in the later nineteenth century were less than half this length.

The absence of half or whole days is another serious difference. Dyer Ball describes '…a listless round, which knew no Sunday rest, nor Wednesday, nor Saturday half-holiday: a Chinese school was for work, and not play; play was considered a waste of time, and, as such, to be discouraged as much as possible: no variety of studies; nothing to break the monotony from daylight till dark, only enough time to take meals being allowed.'[1] Williams also describes the absence of longer holidays. 'The vacations during the year are few; the longest is before new year, at which time the engagement is completed, and the school closes, to be reopened after the teacher and parents have made a new arrangement. The common festivals, of which there are a dozen or more, are regarded as holydays, and form very necessary relaxations in a country destitute of the rest of the Sabbath.'[2]

English schools have often had playgrounds – and the elite schools have had extensive playing fields. Certainly these were enormously important at both the Dragon and Sedbergh and important at Oxford. But they were absent in French schools of the C19 according to Taine, and seem to have been absent in China. One effect is noted by Dyer Ball. 'In England, schools are a nuisance to their neighbours at play-time; there was no

---

1 DYER BALL, *Things Chinese*, p. 207.

2 WILLIAMS, *The Middle Kingdom*, 1, p. 526.

play-time in Chinese schools – they were, on the contrary, a nuisance when the boys were at their lessons.'³

* * *

At the end of the first stage of Chinese traditional education, aged about ten, many children would leave school for good. They had been inculcated over three or so years in very basic skills in reading, if not necessarily understanding, numerous characters. And they had been subjected to a considerable indoctrination in moral instruction. For example, Williams states that :

> '*The importance of filial and fraternal duties are then inculcated by precept and example, to which succeeds a synopsis of the various prince of learning in an ascending series, underseveral heads of numbers; the three great powers, the fourseasons and four cardinal points, the five elements and five constant virtues....*'

The sort of precepts they are learning are as follows:

> '*there are three powers, – heaven, earth, and man.*
> *There are three lights, – the sun, moon, and stars.*
> *There are three bonds, – between prince and minister, justice;*
> *Between father and son, affection; between man and wife, concord.*
> *...Mutual affection of father and son, concord of man and wife;*
> *The older brother's kindness, the younger one's respect;*

---

3 Dyer Ball, *Things Chinese*, p. 207.

Order between seniors and juniors, friendship among associates;
On the prince's part regard, on the minister's true loyalty; –
These ten moral duties are ever binding among men.'[1]

* * *

The system which Confucius systematized had two main goals. Both of them are behind the description above. One is to provide an ethical and moral training for the whole population. The other is more specialized and only occurs in the higher stages of the system, namely to train people for the bureaucracy.

In a country without an institutionalized clerical class there was no emphasis on religious training, a mainstay of western education. There was morality, ethics, but no monotheistic religion.

Without a legal class, lawyers, barristers, judges, magistrates, and the whole panoply of either Roman or Common law, another central role of western education was missing. The Mandarins performed judicial functions as part of their administrative duties, they were not trained specifically for this.

Without a separate military aristocracy and hence a need for soldiers (and sailors) there was no need for a training in military skills to be deployed around the empire. Without uni-versities and third level education, there was no need for the training of academics. Without a wealthy oligarchy of large businessmen and traders, there was no need for this kind of training of capitalists.

The Chinese educational system had only one function in terms of professional training. It was to train civil servants at

---

1 WILLIAMS, *The Middle Kingdom*, 1, p. 528.

all levels of the hierarchy – village leaders, district administrators, provincial leaders, imperial advisors. It was a machine to service a vast bureaucratic Empire and to hold it together. This was one of its manifest functions. This gave it a special feeling, similar to the feeling I have had at times in relation to Oxbridge education for the 'Mandarins' of the British civil service (or previously of the elite of the Indian Civil Service). Dyer Ball puts it thus:

> '...*those wonderful essays, where the reasoning proceeded in a circle, and ended where it began, which were valuable as preparing the student for the Civil Service examinations; this last being the final stage for which all the preceding had been preparatory; this, the goal which had necessitated all the arduous toil, with, in the event of success, its resultant office-holding...*'[2]

---

2 DYER BALL, *Things Chinese*, p. 208.

Conclusion

NINE

Some Benefits and Costs of Modernity

CHINA IS NOW facing a situation unprecedented in its history. For the last five thousand years its great civilization has been based on a vertical (Confucian) system of superiors and inferiors (parent – children, men – women, Emperor – subjects, Mandarins – Peasants). This has been based on groups in which the individual is less important than the group and only has a meaning in relation to another or others.

It is now encountering something entirely different, mainly emanating from the Anglo-American area, or 'Anglosphere.' This is based on an equal set of relations between individuals with innate human rights. In order to see what has happened and what the choices for China are, it is worth examining what has happened in the west over the last few hundred years. What is the world which China is facing, and in particular, what are its advantages and its costs?

* * *

Looked at from the perspective of all human history and all other human civilizations, what has happened during the last three hundred years in the west is extraordinary. A new kind of civilization has emerged which has an unprecedented set of organizational principles.

Most past civilizations have been based on the principles of an ordering of institutional parts in a birth-given order of superiority and inferiority. There was a strict vertical hierarchy, some form of stratification where orders were integrated through a set of levels, whether castes or the opposition between the highly educated and the mass of barely literate population.

Yet the overturning of these premises is precisely what has happened in the last three hundred years and anarchy, on the whole, has not ensued. This is part of the tendency towards equality which Tocqueville analysed. That this happened raises two great questions. How did such a strange thing as the breakdown of hierarchy occur, and how could a civilization not based on it work? What could hold equal people together and prevent them either from falling apart into atomistic confusion or, equally dangerously, from surrendering their liberty to some form of absolutist government?

Put in another way, the problem could be seen in terms of the loss of the sovereignty of groups. In the long history of mankind, people had always existed as subordinate to groups, but now, for the first time, a world arose where the individual came before the group. This is often seen as the quintessence of modern liberty. Again this poses the double question of how such a strange situation could have emerged, and, once present, how it could possibly work. Too much atomization would surely lead to the collapse of the social system. This was one of the great quandaries for the anthropology and sociology of the 19th century and lay behind many of its best-known theories.

* * *

If, basically, the essence of modernity is an ever-vigilant patrolling of the borders between spheres, one is left with those problems of living in an 'Open Society' which many, including poets such as Blake and Yeats, or political philosophers such as Popper, have documented. People are often forced to live in a desiccated world of compromises. They cannot afford to let any particular drive win out for long. All power tends to corrupt, so power must be muzzled. Kinship loyalties and warmth must be held in check and love can seldom be unreserved. Belief and ritual must be tempered and all ethical judgments are provisional and relativistic. Even the pursuit of wealth has to be moderated and many areas are put 'out of bounds.' All knowledge is provisional, all action is tempered by the knowledge of its hidden cost.

The benefits of this modern world are huge: personal liberty and autonomy, an equality of sorts, and wealth undreamed of for vast numbers of people. The consumer revolution deadens the pain of the loss of integration and meaning and few would go back. But the costs are only just below the surface and when a prophet arises who promises the re-integration of life, the overcoming of alienation and anomie, the togetherness of a purpose, whether a Mao, Hitler or Pol Pot, many are ready to abandon their somewhat dry lives of efficiency in order to surrender to the new wholeness. Or they may be attracted to the ecstasies and loss of self of a new Pentecostal religion or New Age faith. For most, however, there are only oases of togetherness, in drink, friendship, sport, music and the institutions of civil society. Much of life is lived in restraint and rational balance.

As well as the costs to the inner core of the modern world, there are the costs incurred as this world spreads outwards, undermining all closed systems through its conspicuous economic success or military might. Local worlds of meaning are drained and a technocratic, managerial, ascetic world partially replaces them. One recompense is the dream of material wealth and leisure. Another is constituted by the forms of associationalism in sport, business, religion and elsewhere which partially overcomes the separateness of the lonely crowd. With the fall of communism, the only surviving holistic world system offering an alternative to the Open Society is Islam.

To many of its critics the modern world is fairly repulsive morally, and psychologically almost intolerable. Yet others believe that it is the worst of all possible systems, except for all the rest, which are even worse. The hedonism, loneliness, lack of purpose, contradictions are unattractive, but the world of communistic, fascistic or other totalitarian systems are even less attractive in the long run both at the personal level and in terms of what they produce. Liberty, equality and the pursuit of happiness may not encompass all the lofty goals humans can pursue, but there are worse. The modern world that emerged over the long centuries has turned humans into great lords of all things, yet they remain a prey to all, including their own inner self-doubt.

All of this means that humans are not blissfully happy in our modern world. It has a number of the properties of anomie, alienation, loneliness, coldness described by a great many authors. In particular the individual is held in perpetual doubt. Every action has a cost as well as a benefit, enthusiasm can be crushed, there are no certainties. This is one of the great attractions of play, art and romantic love, a moment of re-integration and meaning. Usually one has to settle for a compromise between almost equally balanced loyalties and demands. Yet the balancing of them and the constant contradictions are probably also the cause of the energy of modern civilization. Some kind of fission or explosion occurs again and again. It is those societies where fusion has completely dominated which appear to become inert.

*   *   *

If, as Tonniës put it, the opposition is between societies based on contract, reason, the mind, in other words *gesellschaft* (or what Maitland translated accurately not as 'association,' but 'partnership'), as opposed to societies based on emotion, status, blood and place, or gemeinschaft (community) then modern civilizations, in order to work and be tolerable places to live in, have somehow to find a way to fuse the two. This is what 'fellowship' or trust does. It is vaguely related to clubism, to 'matiness' in the Australian sense, but is not gendered. It makes it possible to set up meaningful, enduring, sub-communities within a basically contractual society. These 'communities' are not based on blood and place, but communities of sentiment as well as purely instrumental and practical goals, which make life worth living and complex co-operation possible. Whether a music club, a rowing club, a ballroom dancing club, a gardening club, a political club, a religious fraternity, a business organization, a charity, or a thousand other organizations, the blend of heart and mind, of emotion and reason, of the short-term instrumental and the long-term affections, of self-love and social, can be achieved.

It is this invention of associational institutions which explains why most of the major charitable, social, political as well as economic, political and sporting associations were invented in England. The list would include the RSPCA, Salvation Army, Lions clubs, Boy Scouts and Girl Guides, Oxfam, Women's Institutes, Rambler's Associations and so on almost endlessly. And as Tocqueville had noticed, participation in such self-governing associations are the main bulwarks against dictatorship. The rights of associations are the protection for liberty and all totalitarian aspirants try to curtail them, usually on the pretext of war or the threat of war.

The real mystery is how such anomalous and mixed entities could arise; with too much sentiment to have been achieved by contract alone, with too much choice and reason to be ascribed purely by status. They are logical contradictions, hybrid forms, as Maitland so elegantly described. They are corporate, having bodies, yet not incorporated by the State. They are formally constituted, artificial entities, yet evoking the passionate adherence of their members. Do they have any parallels in the higher animals, one wonders, that is associations based on mutual interest and proven capacities independent of birth ? Some have lasted up to eight hundred years in the West, the Universities, Inns of Court, religious brotherhoods, guilds and fraternities. Yet the great time of their proliferation was probably the seventeenth to nineteenth centuries when Britain became the richest and most powerful nation in the world. And the whole art of setting up these quasi-groups was exported to America.

This is not to argue that such an associational world had

never occurred before or outside the Anglo-American region. This situation of numerous non-kinship, non-state associations is what was characteristic of the small-scale communities of Western Europe in the early medieval period. Thousands of semi-contractual, semi-permanent institutions, religious fraternities, guilds, craft mysteries, liberties, vills and manors, feudal associations, universities were present. It was a community of communities.

This was, to a certain extent, also the situation in medieval Japan after the collapse of the Chinese-based civilization in the eleventh and twelfth centuries. Numerous semi-contractual associations of a religious and secular kind flourished. Such periods, as in the free cities of southern Germany or Renaissance Italy, are periods of enormous innovation and energy. Yet they usually do not last for long. The parts are knitted up together, the loose confederations and liberties crushed, a few powerful institutions, Leviathan and the Papacy, grow and absorb smaller entities until there is a new hierarchical and holistic world. This happened in different ways in ancien regime Europe and Tokugawa Japan. They were alike in seeing a move away from contract to status. In only one or two exceptional cases, for example Holland, parts of Scandinavia, England, does one see a move from contract and status to something beyond both of them, namely trust and association.

In continental Europe, with its revived Roman Law from the 14th century, the new institutions found it difficult to survive and have several times almost been snuffed out in the twentieth century. Likewise it has been difficult for them to take hold in communist states, which consider all alternatives to the Party with deadly hostility. Nor have they always found great favour in caste-based India or, until recently, in much of Latin America. Only in Japan, where the legacy of medieval feudalism was a society already curiously modern in its separations, even if overlaid with the rigidities imposed after the Tokugawa gained dominance in the early seventeenth century, could the Anglo-American system rapidly take root, even if it was again temporarily repressed in the period up to the Second World War.

These associations blend with a modern world in various ways. Firstly, they tend to fit within a separated sphere. Whereas the traditional spheres tried to be hegemonic, for example kinship dominated religion and the economy, or politics tried to organize the rest, the associations were located within a particular sphere. A religious sect should not interfere much in politics or the market, a gardening club would not pronounce on religion, a sporting club should not tamper with the market. So these associations did not demand a total, but rather a partial, goal-directed, loyalty. On the other hand, they tended to be more than purely utilitarian. They had rules, demanded commitment, excluded as well as included, had a feeling of community, that is to say of belonging. The call to efficiency in pursuit of certain ends, sport, thought, politics, worship, could be heeded. Yet the individual could also have a sense of mutual friendship, fellowship, meaning, social appreciation in Smith's terms. So the whole was more than the sum of the parts.

As far as the relations between these associational groups go, this was flexible, fluid and quite relaxed. There was sometimes games-like competition, as in a college or university boat race. There was sometimes ranking. But on the whole the structure was maintained, as in other acephalous (headless) systems by the tension between the groups. In the same way, the system as a whole worked through structural tensions and contradictions and oppositions, rather than through a merging of top-downwards authority.

Thus, in theory, through the mysterious contradictions of these new mixed forms of association, the individual can expand beyond the isolation of the lonely crowd, to become part of numerous quasi-groups, the fellowship stretching from transitory ones (the pub or communal hot spring) to an enduring group making or doing things together over the years. Even if each woman and man is not part of a continent, in theory each person can visit islands of fellowship in a sea of atomistic, contractual, market society. This possibility, and the resolution of the logical contradiction of self-love and social, is the mysterious essence of modernity.

In a trick which is so difficult to understand, a civilization has emerged which has separated off different parts of life, the institutions of power (politics), wealth (economics), knowledge and belief (religion), warmth and procreation (kinship). But the intolerable burden of living in such a world, the enormous inefficiency of a world of isolated, non-trusting, individuals who would be the only locus of contact between the separated spheres, is overcome by a new flexible institution, whose prototype was the trust. This is something akin to the reciprocal altruism of the biologists, but with humans is much more than that, and develops into an extraordinary mixture of flexibility and commitment, of individual and community, of calculation (reason) and loyalty (emotion). This is what gave Maitland hope that a new world which combined liberty, equality and wealth was both possible and might continue and underlay Fukuzawa's strategies for founding a new Japan.

* * *

All this focuses the problem for China. It wants to use the best of the west – in particular the advanced technologies, elements of the economic and social system, some features of western law and educational theory. On the other hand, how is it to fit a traditionally vertical system of relationships with a basically lateral system of contracting individuals? In some ways it has considerable advantages in doing this in that the traditional Confucian social structure was based on an open system of access to all positions through examination. It has also been forced to break down the large groupings of the traditional family system, so that most people now have far less dense relations with distant kin. So it has a great deal of flexibility and has always been very 'rational' in its attitude towards religion and belief.

So there is a chance for China to develop a new kind of civilization, not as with Japan a surface of the west, and a deep structure of ancient Japan, but one which is more integrated and consistent. Yet in order to do this, it obviously has to keep a number of its historical cultural features which gives it a special identity. In order to achieve this difficult task, the more it understands what has developed in the west and is on offer, not just in science and technology and education, but in the deep core of western institutions, the better.

So I have not attempted in these short letters to solve China's problems. But I have tried to make the choices more visible, to underline the contradictions, and to highlight how two very different systems are now trying to live alongside each other.

I do this because I greatly admire China and find in my young Chinese friends an open willingness to try to puzzle out solutions to their predicament. I also admire the great history of China and its care for the old, for the other, and for culture. I believe it has a huge amount to offer to an often over-materialistic and over-individualistic west. So, as it grows in confidence and force, I believe it could shape the west as much as the west shapes it. And in the process both civilizations need to be true to their historical identity, but to understand and share enough to promote peace, tolerance and mutual support. This is already happening and I wish you all success in the further adventure.

Alan Macfarlane

How We Understand the World

THIS BOOK IS part of a series of short letters written to young friends. Encouraged by the reception of my *Letters to Lily* (2005), I decided to write a set of letters to her younger sister – Reflections for Rosa. I was then asked by other friends to write short books for their children.

In each I try to explore some aspect of 'How We Understand the World,' based on my experience as an anthropologist and historian at Cambridge University. I have tried to put into simple words what I have learnt about discovery, creativity and methods to understand our complex world.

EXPLORE THE SERIES

1. How to Discover the World *Reflections for Rosa*
2. How to Investigate Mysteries *Secrets for Sam*
3. How to Study the World *Suggestions for Shuo*
4. How do We Know *Advice for April*
5. How to Understand Each Other *Notes for Nina*
6. The Survival Manual *Thoughts for Taras*
7. A Modern Education *Advice for Ariston*
8. Learning to be Modern *Jottings for James*
9. Intelligent Machines *Conversations with Gerry*

Image on front cover is an adaptation of Children's Games by Pieter Bruegel the Elder, available in the public domain.

www.ingramcontent.com/pod-product-compliance
Lightning Source LLC
Chambersburg PA
CBHW061325040426
42444CB00011B/2781